RHODE
ISLAND
LEGENDS

RHODE ISLAND LEGENDS

Haunted Hallows & Monsters' Lairs

M.E. Reilly-McGreen

Charleston | London

THE
History
PRESS

Published by The History Press
Charleston, SC 29403
www.historypress.net

Cover illustration: *Werewolf von Neuses*, circa 1685. *PD-US*.
Back cover black-and-white photo by Daniel G. Dunn.

First published 2012

Manufactured in the United States

ISBN 978.1.60949.477.3

Library of Congress CIP data applied for.

Notice: The information in this book is true and complete to the best of our knowledge. It is offered without guarantee on the part of the author or The History Press. The author and The History Press disclaim all liability in connection with the use of this book.

For Tara Reilly Sanda and Mag Ryan, brave girls both.

The greatest trick the devil ever played was convincing the world that he did not exist.

—Charles Baudelaire

Contents

Acknowledgements   11

Introduction   13

A Guide to Where Not to Go in Rhode Island   23

PART I. HAUNTED HALLOWS

The Crying Rocks   29

The Cursed Opal   30

The Portrait of Judge Potter   36

The Queens of Belcourt Castle   40

The Treasure of Carbuncle Pond   43

Tuggie Bannocks and the Witch Sheep   46

How Mark Dodge Stilled the Dancing Mortar   52

The Moaning Bones of Mount Tom   55

Another Tale of a Restless Spirit with an Axe to Grind   56

The One Who Got Away?   57

A Tale of Nine Men's Misery   60

The Last Voyage of the *Seabird*   61

CONTENTS

PART II. MONSTERS' LAIRS

A Visit to the Shunned House — 63

Welcome to Chariho: Rhode Island's Roswell — 70

The Tale of the Crying Bog — 74

How the Devil Came to Do God's Work — 79

The Devil and Old Richard Corey — 84

The Unfortunate Hannah Robinson — 90

An Incident at Dark Swamp — 96

Lair of the Loup Garou — 104

Mrs. Jencks's Ghost — 106

Narragansett: The Lost Atlantis — 111

She Who Shall Not Be Named — 115

Watching and Waiting for You — 117

Selected Bibliography — 125

About the Author — 127

Acknowledgements

Thank you Joseph, Reilly, Colin and Peter for being the great men you are. Thank you Mom and Dad for being you. To Anna, thank you for introducing me to Mike and Sue Hazard, who were so gracious in allowing me to visit and talk to them about Hannah Robinson. Mike and Sue, it was a pleasure to hear your Hannah stories. Betty Cotter, you remain the best mentor a person could have. Dan Dunn, thank you for an amazing cover shot. To the ladies of the Kingston and Peace Dale libraries, thank you always. Thanks to The History Press's Jeff Saraceno, Jaime Muehl and Dani McGrath for your hard work. And, kick butt, Missy Cook Stark.

Introduction

BRAVE GIRLS KNOW THE OGRE NEVER DIES

Part One of My Adventures with The History Channel Film Crew

It was the spring of 2008. The day was warm, and I was waiting, alone, in a sun-dappled wood, sitting on a bed of pine needles on a hill in a cemetery in Woonsocket. Surrounding me were weathered old headstones, worn with time but still beautiful things bearing carvings of elegant weeping willows and Grecian urns.

I was awaiting a crew from The History Channel, which was filming an episode for a television series called *Monster Quest*. The show's goal was to explore the scientific, logical explanations for a legend's birth and growth. This particular show's topic was New England's vampire tradition. Both the crew and I were following Michael Bell, PhD, esteemed folklorist and author of the book *Food for the Dead: On the Trail of New England's Vampires*. The crew was filming Michael; I was writing about the crew filming Michael.

The crew was supposed to be at the graveyard at 3:30 p.m., filming at the very spot where I sat. It was to be the culmination of a two-day shoot of the state's vampire hotspots. Yes, Rhode Island has more than one. But it was just me and the headstones two hours after the appointed time. One headstone, you see, was very special. It was genuine, physical evidence of a bona fide vampire in residence.

Young Simon Whipple Aldrich died in 1841. He was twenty-seven years old. Inscribed on his headstone, after the usual information, were the words:

> *Altho' consumption's vampire grasp*
> *Had seized thy mortal frame*

And then...nothing.

The last two lines of the headstone had been obscured by concrete. I assumed the concrete was the work of some Good Samaritan trying to protect the headstone from vandals. Exeter's famed vampire Mercy Brown also had cement and an iron band anchoring her headstone firmly in place. It struck me as ironic that the two lines should be obliterated, but premature endings, I've learned, are a common motif in vampire lore.

It occurred to me that, if I were to believe the inscription, I was sitting in front of the headstone of a vampire. In the woods. Alone. Nearing sunset. No matter that I didn't believe in vampires or monsters. Under such circumstances, the supernatural seems possible, and noises likely made by birds and squirrels have a way of sounding like the undead advancing upon the unsuspecting.

Exsanguination—it would be an ironic, fitting and oddly comic end to a lifetime's love affair with monsters but a tragically abrupt end to my five-month career as a vampire hunter. But more about that later. First, I would tell you about how I came to be interested in writing about ghosts, ghouls and other monsters.

HOW TO SURVIVE THE OGRE

I have a Sunday ritual that I observe faithfully. "Spooky Movie Sunday" is my day to watch horror films. Neither my sons nor my husband have any interest in horror films, so I'm on my own. It's getting harder and

Headstone of Mercy Brown. *Photo by author.*

harder to find a really good horror movie, though. Most are ridiculous or, worse, pathetic. You know the ones: all blood, no plot.

Those who know their horror movies know their tropes. I'd violated one of the most basic in going alone to the Woonsocket cemetery. Big no-no—so much so that if I were watching a heroine in a movie do the same, I'd be shaking my head and muttering about people too stupid to live.

For those who aren't familiar with the other inviolable rules that must be followed to survive a horror movie, I'll give you a quick primer. It's my variation on a popular list that I'll title "Things You Never, Ever Do in a Horror Movie If You Want to Live." So, don't

- go up to the attic, down to the basement or into a forest, graveyard or abandoned house, church or factory. And never,

ever leave the car. People who get separated from the pack get picked off. The same rules that apply on elementary school field trips apply in horror movies: Stay with your group. Have a buddy. Don't go off alone.

- say, "I'll be right back" because you won't. The guy or gal who tries to play the hero early on never makes it to the end of the movie. Better to be very, very scared. Leave the heroics to the football player.

- lose your virginity. Another reason for abstinence, kiddos, is psycho killers tend to spare the innocent when they go on their bloody rampages.

- let your gas tank get to empty. Too many movie teens have been eviscerated or decapitated because they couldn't be bothered to fill up their gas tanks before heading out for the night. Use your head while you still have it.

- hang out with the head cheerleader or the captain of the football team. Really, anyone wearing any kind of varsity jacket or carrying pom-poms will get killed brutally and quickly. Psycho killers find those types just as annoying as the rest of us do.

- build or buy a house on a Native American burial ground, take a job at an isolated grand hotel or rent a former funeral home. There are some things that should never, ever be disturbed, people. Native American burial grounds top the list, and the others should just be common sense.

- play with an Ouija board. Demonic possession. Duh.

- enter a creepy old home, abandoned mental hospital (like Exeter's Ladd Center) or suspicious-looking house of worship to escape the monster. This is the monster's lair. This is where he's been wanting to get you for the entire length of the film.

- be mean to the shy, smart brunette girl. She's going to live. Why? A) She's inevitably the virgin of the group. B) She's not dumb. C) She not blond. It's not fair, but if you're dumb or blond or a dumb blonde, you're toast.

- ever assume you've killed the monster. Because, as all brave brunettes know, the ogre never dies.

What's interesting about horror movies is how much they owe to fairy tales—my first and still favorite literary genre. I especially loved fairy tale heroines. The young-but-brave girl goes on a perilous journey and is threatened by various malevolent magical objects and monstrous creatures. She suffers setbacks, like poison apples that lodge in the throat, spindle pricks that put her in a one-hundred-year coma or rotten husbands who lock her in a tower, saying they'll kill her if she doesn't spin a roomful of straw into gold by morning. I would read those stories with mounting apprehension, thinking, *No! No! No, don't do that! Don't eat that! Don't go there! Don't open the door to the room you were forbidden to enter; he's got all his dead wives in there!*

But no worries. Happy endings are a given in fairy tales, right? Nope. *The Complete Fairy Tales of the Brothers Grimm* came my way in a collection of old books my grandmother gave me. And were they filled with happily-ever-afters? Oh, no. Not at all. Some heroes and heroines in these stories have their limbs cut off and their eyes poked out. Stepmothers decapitate their sons and make stews from their flesh. Daughters flee incestuous fathers. Not the happy-happy ending but rather the fate-worse-than-death outcome.

I was enthralled by these dark tales. Once upon a time didn't always end in happily ever after? Wow. In adulthood, my fascination for fairy tales extended to stories I heard of Rhode Island men and women who found themselves in the realm of the supernatural. I began to collect the stories, much like the Brothers Grimm did two hundred years ago, visiting places, talking to people and recording the stories. And some of what I've found, I share here.

What you'll find here is the best of Rhode Island legends and lore, a who's who of monsters, including aliens, vampires, witches, ghosts, fairies and werewolves. Even the Greek gods make an appearance. And you'll also learn of some rather remarkable magical objects: a dancing mortar, a cursed opal, a cellar of the damned and library books that check themselves out.

Collecting and recording these stories has been a true pleasure and a real adventure. In the interest of full disclosure, some tales are an amalgamation of different, and sometimes conflicting, versions of the

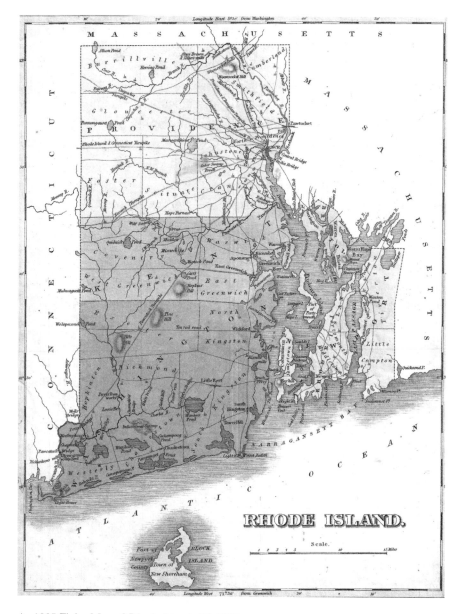

An 1827 Finley Map of Rhode Island. *PD 1923.*

same story. Some stories were delivered orally. And while all the tales recounted here have their roots in legitimate Rhode Island folklore, I've chosen to use the folklore to underpin narratives rather than present them in the reportorial style of much historical prose.

The Hermit's House, Narragansett. *Photo by Daniel G. Dunn.*

INTERVIEW WITH A WARLOCK

Part Two of My Adventures with The History Channel Film Crew

The overcast skies let go over the old Connecticut graveyard at about ten o'clock in the morning. I stood with a Connecticut museum curator, out of the camera shot, and watched one of the Department of Agriculture scientists walk the cemetery with this large, red rectangular tool at her hip. This machine measured disturbances of soil well beneath the carpet of grass we walked on. And if this high-tech-dirt-disturbance detector should find something unusual, it might just be evidence that people unearthed their dead to mutilate them postmortem in an effort to rid themselves of the vampires they were sure lived in the bodies.

I felt before I saw the man who crept up behind me. He wore a bright blue plastic poncho, the kind that could do double duty as a dropcloth. Greasy locks of gray hair hung to his shoulders. He grinned—a not entirely pleasant expression. Perhaps, though, it was his appearance that lent the air of menace. The unshaven face. The disheveled clothing. And the man's teeth. Tiny gray and brown headstones, they were broken, uneven and set at odd angles.

"What are you doing?" he asked. I explained about The History Channel, *Monster Quest*, the various people and their roles in the drama. Poncho man sneered.

"There's no vampires here. If there were, I would know."

I was intrigued. "How?"

"I live here. With the ghosts. They would've told me."

The time had come for me to edge away.

"Do you know what I am? Do you know what a warlock is?"

"A male witch?"

"That's right," said the warlock. He smiled, flashing his graveyard teeth. "That means you can tell me your secrets."

I declined his generous offer but thanked him and then lied. I was part of the crew, I said. I was needed on the set.

Rhode Island's master of the macabre H.P. Lovecraft made the Ocean State the setting of many a dark tale. *Photo by author.*

Close-up of the H.P. Lovecraft memorial. *Photo by author.*

The warlock reached beneath his poncho. It was a tense moment. There was no telling what he might have hidden there or what he might expose. Then, with a magician's flourish, he produced a can of Bud Ice. He cracked the flip top and gulped, then offered me some. I felt I had stepped into a Stephen King movie. This was the crypt keeper, Dracula's Renfield, Lovecraft's Joseph Curwen, Young Frankenstein's Igor offering me a sip of his beer at ten thirty in the morning. I declined. My chivalrous warlock then bowed and returned to the woods. I smiled. I'd come to the graveyard in search of vampires and found a warlock.

And I was reminded again of why I loved my work—it's for just such experiences and the stories they yield. I hope these stories of monsters and magical objects are as enjoyable to read as they are for me to relate.

A Guide to Where Not to Go in Rhode Island

Heard a good ghost story lately? Better yet, lived one?
I asked Chariho Regional High School students that question on the first day of my class "Rhode Island Myth, Folklore and Legend." I'd just shared with them that their very school was smack-dab in the heart of alien country. Wood River Junction is Rhode Island's Roswell. It was just the first of many revelations for the students. Many did not know, for instance, that Rhode Island has more vampires per capita than any other state in the country. And that Bigfoot is said to roam the nearby Great Swamp.

Occasionally, I was happily surprised to find that my students had stories of their own. Like this one shared by star student Jennifer Damicis:

> *I cannot honestly say that I've heard any alien stories others than what I've read in books. Of those, none of them were related to Rhode Island. However, I do have a small werewolf story that excited me. I live in an area surrounded by Nature Conservancy land. I've been hiking and exploring the property since I was five. My parents had always warned my brother and I of coyotes and fisher cats, but never had we seen any. One night, as my family was on our way to our house, we were driving through a densely wooded area. In the headlights we saw what looked like what is best described as a "Harry Potter–like" werewolf. On two feet, an animal with long, slender limbs sprinted across the road. It was covered in fur and was faster than any human. It had a dog-like face.*

A contemporary report of a werewolf roaming the southernmost part of the state. Jen's story was a rare gift that I treasured then and now.

I collect stories like other people do stamps, coins or shoes. Nothing makes me happier than to discover a nearly lost tale or to hear a credible contemporary tell me of something he or she witnessed. Here, I've provided a quick-and-easy reference guide to the best places in the state to haunt and be haunted by monsters, gods and aliens. Details as to exact lair locations vary. And this is by no means an exhaustive list.

Happy hunting. If anything unusual happens, please let me know.

ALIENS (BEST BETS): Wood River Junction, Providence, Newport County, Cumberland
BIGFOOT: the Great Swamp, South Kingstown
BLEEDING ROCKS: Indian Corner, Slocumville, North Kingstown
CLASSICAL GODS AND GODDESSES AT PLAY: Narragansett Beach, Narragansett; Worden's Pond, South Kingstown
CRYING ROCKS: Child Crying Rocks, Charlestown

The Great Swamp, South Kingstown. *Photo by author.*

The Towers, Narragansett. *Photo by author.*

Worden's Pond, South Kingstown. *Photo by author.*

Van Wickle Gates, Brown University, Providence. Horror master H.P. Lovecraft was haunted by his failure to attend this prestigious university. *Photo by author.*

CURSED MATCHING THRONES: the Salt Chairs of Belcourt Castle, Newport

THE DEVIL: Devil's Hole, Woonsocket; Devil's Ring, Peace Dale

THE DEVIL'S HOOFPRINT: Devil's Foot Rock, North Kingstown; Purgatory Chasm, Newport

FAIRIES: Worden's Pond, South Kingstown

FLESH-EATING VEGETATION: Roger William's Root, Providence

GHOSTS OF FAMOUS HORROR WRITERS: Edgar Allan Poe, Benefit Street, Providence; H.P. Lovecraft, Barnes Street and Swan Point Cemetery, Providence

GIANT WOLVES AND BLACK SHUCK: Devil's Hole, Woonsocket; Fort Wetherill, Jamestown; Wolf Rocks, Exeter; Wolf Bog, Peace Dale

HAUNTED ASYLUMS: the Ladd Center, Exeter

HAUNTED HOLY SITES: the Monastery, Cumberland

HAUNTED MILLS: Slater Mill, Pawtucket; Ramtail Factory, Foster; Moorsefield Road, Kingston

HAUNTED WEDDING VENUES: Sprague Mansion, Cranston

Headless Ghost Horse: Belmont Avenue, Wakefield

Ghost Regiments: Route 138, Kingston; Hessian Hole, Portsmouth

Ghost Ships: Beavertail, Jones's Ledge, Jamestown; Grave's Point, Jamestown; the *Seabird*, Newport; the *Palantine*, Block Island

Headless Human Ghosts: Indian Corner, North Kingstown; Moorsefield Road, South Kingstown

It: Dark Swamp, Chepachet

Jewelry-Wearing Giant Serpents: Wilson's Woods, South Kingstown; Carbuncle Pond, Coventry

Moaning Bones: Arcadia; Narragansett

Orbs: Charlestown, Rhode Island

Pirates' Ghosts: Gravelly Point, Newport

Pirates' Treasure: Block Island; Sugarloaf Hill, South Kingstown

Possessed Paintings: Kingston Free Library, Kingston

The Fleur de Lys House, Providence. *Photo by author.*

Saints' Relics: Rough Point, Newport

Sea Monsters: Block Island; Point Judith, Narragansett

Skeletons in Armor: Old Stone Mill, Newport

Skulking Monks: Belcourt Castle, Newport; Nine Men's Misery, Cumberland

Soldiers' Spirits: Hessian Hole, Portsmouth; Kingston Village, Kingston; Nine Men's Misery, Cumberland

Tragic Maidens' Spirits: Hannah Robinson, Hannah Robinson's Tower and Rock, South Kingstown; Dolly Cole, Dolly Cole's Brook, Foster; Angela O'Leary, Fleur de Lys House, Providence

Vampires: Chestnut Hill Cemetery, Exeter; Mooresfield, South Kingstown; Plain Meeting House, West Greenwich; the Shunned House, Benefit Street, Providence

Wailing Knight: Belcourt Castle, Newport

Wailing Woman: The Crying Bog, Narragansett

Wandering Wraiths: Dorothy's Hollow, Narragansett

Werewolves: the Great Swamp, Charlestown; Woonsocket; Watson's Corner, South Kingstown

Witches: Benefit Street, Providence; Chestnut Hill Cemetery, Exeter; Hell Hollow, North Kingstown; Hopkins Hill, East Greenwich; Kettle Hollow, North Kingstown; Ministerial Woods, South Kingstown; Witches Altar, Narragansett; Westerly

Part I

Haunted Hallows

THE CRYING ROCKS

They're said to be at the edge of the cedar swamp, in the woods of Charlestown, north of the old Narragansett Indian schoolhouse, near School House Pond, where John Onion skated with the devil himself. The Crying Rocks, the old people say, are glacial rocks that ring with the cries of babies. Narragansett mothers tell their children to stay away.

It's a cursed, dark place, the site of so much evildoing that Nature herself recoils. It is evil that has caused the cedars' bark to curl in on itself. It is evil that has stained the rhododendrons' centers with crimson sprays of blood. Fearful they'll be discovered, the spruce trees whisper their warnings: "Go, back. Leave this place."

Here, the Narragansett John Paul told Ezra Stiles, terrible things were done to children, infants. Children born of unwed mothers, children born with infirmities or handicaps—such children were left out there in the woods to die or be killed outright. It was just the order of things back then, a way to keep the people strong. The weakness of one threatened the survival of all, the elders taught.

It's said that once upon a time you could see a mass of little skeletons, their fragile bones bleached white in the sun. But now all traces of their physical bodies have long disappeared.

But something of those babies survives still.

If you should visit this place in the early morning, between the hours of 2:00 and 3:00 a.m., when the spirits are at their most restless, you can hear their cries.

Though you may wish you hadn't.

THE CURSED OPAL

The opal changed colors with the slightest movement of her finger, and she lost track of time just looking at it. It seemed alive, a world unto itself, and it outshone even the tiny diamonds that surrounded it. Bell said it was his mother's and her mother's before that, and he'd promised her he'd give it to the woman who would be his wife.

Was she that woman? She could see the pain—and was that anger?—in his eyes when she strung it on a silver chain and tucked it safely out of sight, under her shirt. She checked her reflection in the dirty glass of his window and adjusted her silk blouse so that not even the faintest outline of the ring was visible.

"There," she said to herself.

Even with her back to Bell, she could sense his disapproval and turned to see him scowling at her. If he weren't so handsome, if she weren't so wild about him, she might be scared. But his jealousy thrilled her. She crossed the room and sat on his lap. He was a bear of a man with the bearing of an aristocrat. She felt frail in his arms, a thing of little substance or consequence.

"Closer to my heart," she whispered and kissed him.

He snorted. It was a stupid, even heartless thing to say. Things were never easy with Bell. She was already engaged when they met. She thought he'd be happy enough to have a brief affair. He was free of any obligation to her, an almost married, almost respectable woman. But the affair, and her feelings for Bell, had taken her by surprise. She couldn't let him go. She wouldn't.

But she also wasn't ready to let go of the life marriage to a doctor would guarantee her. So when Bell proposed, she took the opal. But she kept her diamond, too. Now, here she was with two fiancés, painfully aware that if she did not make a decision, one would be forced upon her. And she wanted Bell. Desperately. But the doctor—a man whom she'd admired, a man to whom she'd been attracted, a man who loved her— she wanted him, too.

"In time, I'll tell him," she said. She lied.

She just wasn't sure about Bell and their future. He was a sailor—not a captain; not an officer, even—and she wasn't interested in being a sailor's wife. She wasn't going to spend her married life alone, watching the sea, scared at every storm cloud on the horizon. What if he didn't come back? Newport was awash in widows and, worse, sailors' whores. Was she one? Were there women elsewhere waiting for him now? Though she never shared these thoughts with Bell, he knew them.

"We won't be apart. Not ever," he would say. He spoke with an earnestness, an intensity that thrilled her. And scared her, honestly. He was never flirtatious, never lighthearted. She would try to distract him by talking of their wedding, but he wouldn't play with her. Sometimes he even got angry.

"You think this is a game?" he spat. "You have no idea what it's like to see you parading around with your doctor and your father looking so pleased with himself, and I have to act like I don't even know you. You say you're going to be my wife in here, but out there," he inclined his head in the direction of the window, "out there, you're a stranger."

She felt shame then. And, oddly, hopelessness. What would she do?

She took the opal ring off its chain and placed it on her slender finger. A perfect fit. As always, it was an effort to drag her eyes off it. She was bewitched by it. She placed her hands on either side of his face and stared into his hazel eyes. When he was angry, the gold in them seemed brighter. Today, they were like twin suns. She kissed him. It was a hard, desperate kiss—as if that would make a difference to him. She was a fool. He would leave her. What man would allow himself to be treated this way? He would leave. She just knew it. She had to protect herself.

How had it come to this? She had thought she would have a little fun before she married. But she had fallen in love with him.

"I'm sorry," she whispered, wrapping her arms around him. "I'll tell him and my father soon. I promise. I love you."

But when she left that dirty, shabby room where Bell lived, she switched opal for diamond. Though the diamond ring was more impressive and, she suspected, far more valuable, the opal was Bell: mysterious, exotic, mercurial, beautiful. Why did he insist on ruining what they had with this ridiculous dream of marriage? She wanted both rings, both men.

She would have both.

As always, when she tucked the opal into her shirt, the girl felt oddly apologetic, as if the ring knew her intent, her deceit. It's not a person, she chided herself. But hiding it away felt wrong.

"I'm sorry," she said.

And most of the time, she meant it.

If Bell had a first name, no one at Black Shuck's Pub knew it. Some found it curious, though not the wharf rats. Men in Bell's business admired the quiet ones. It usually meant a man was trustworthy, a rare and valuable asset among liars and thieves. No seaman was safe in a city like Newport. One government's privateer was another's pirate. Say the wrong thing to the wrong person and you could end up hanged.

So Bell kept to himself. Mostly. Occasionally, he'd take a pint and join in a hand of cards. But he said little and wagered less. He had little of value, except for that opal ring he kept around his neck. Rumor was he'd stolen it right off the hand of the Spanish King Alfonso XII, the one who went mad after his wife passed—his beloved queen, Maria de las Mercedes, who had died mysteriously the previous year. It was her ring. Spanish sailors were said to cross themselves when they heard tales of the opal. They said it was cursed; it brought death. Most in Bell's company coveted the ring. When it first disappeared, some thought one of the others had stolen it. But Bell would have said something, killed someone. Then they heard Bell had given it to some woman he'd met. Some knew of her. She wasn't a whore, but they suspected she wasn't quite a lady either. And she didn't wear the ring. If she had, she'd probably have lost it—and a finger—by now, they told one another. Everyone who saw that damn thing wanted it.

The day Bell left Newport, a young sailor delivered a note to the woman's home. That evening, after the boy had spent Bell's payment for services rendered on pints, he told those assembled at Black Shuck's what had transpired. The woman had answered the door and greedily grabbed the note from the boy's hand.

"She read it and put her hand to her mouth, like she was trying to stop herself from talking or screaming," he said. "She began to cry, then scream, and she started tearing at the collar of her shirt. It was like she was choking.

"But she wasn't. She was getting at something. She had that ring of Bell's on a chain. And then," the deckhand's eyes widened at the memory, "then she pulled her diamond ring off her finger and threw it like it was trash. She put the opal on her finger."

The boy paused.

"I think it was her father and another man who came in then, and they saw her all upset and her shirt ripped, and they thought I'd done it and drew a gun on me. She stopped them, saying it was over. Saying Bell was the one she wanted. Saying she'd made up her mind, and they wouldn't stop her."

The boy shook his head.

"She screamed, 'I am his!' Then she just ran out. Her father and the man ran after her. I thought about stealing something before I left, but all I took was the note," the deckhand said. "I wanted to see what the note said."

"What did it say?" asked one of the whores who gathered around the boy to hear the story. She looked upset, her eyes wet and glassy with unshed tears. She'd been a favorite of Bell's before he'd met the woman.

"It said, 'Remember me. Always. B.'"

They would see her often, wandering along the wharf, always looking out to sea. She grew thinner, dirtier, more wild looking. In time, she developed a hacking cough, and her handkerchiefs were spotted and then bloomed with blood. Consumption. Her fiancé initially forgave her—she was beautiful, after all, and rich—but all attempts he made to reconcile with her were met with disdain and, eventually, scorn. Her parents tried to reason with her, too. But there was no talking sense into her.

"He will come for me," she said. "I wasn't worthy before. But he will come. I think it will be soon. He said we wouldn't be apart."

"You're horribly mistaken," her mother said. "He left you. He left you, and he's not coming back. You're half dead with pining for him. Would you give him your very life?"

"I would give him my soul," the girl said.

Every time a ship would come into port, she would accost the sailors, clinging to them, begging for news of Bell. Finally, she got her answer: he had died in a squall off the coast of Bermuda. The news of Bell's death devastated her. She had to atone. She left her parents, exchanging the comfort of their home and their love for a brothel and the embrace of strangers. "This is who I really am," she said to her father on their last meeting. "This is all I am good for."

She died alone in an alley, a wraith; her corpse almost unrecognizable to her father and the young doctor whose diamond ring she had thrown away. Instead, on her ring finger, the girl wore the opal. It shown all the more brilliantly sitting on her filthy hand, her stick-like fingers frozen claws. The policeman who found her stopped a young thief in the act of taking a knife to the girl's hand, so desperate was he for the ring. Funny thing, though, neither man was able to pry the ring from the dead girl's finger.

The girl's father thought he buried the cursed ring with her; he did not know that her mother had intervened. As it had her daughter, the opal bewitched the mother. And when she slid it off her daughter's dead hand, she told herself her daughter would find it a sin to bury such a beautiful thing. And it fit her hand so perfectly, the mother thought as she admired the opal. She could look at its colors change for hours.

When the dead man came to the door asking that his ring be returned to him, the mother thought about lying. It would have been so easy to say that the ring had been lost or stolen or sold. But something about the man made it impossible for her to follow through with her plan.

"The ring is mine," Bell said. "I did not give it to you. She did not give it to you. You must give it to me. I have promised it to another."

"You've forgotten her so soon?"

"No," Bell said. "She is always with me as long as I carry the ring."

"But you said you're going to give my daughter's engagement ring to another woman."

"Yes," Bell said. "But she will become *my* wife, and the ring will remain *mine*."

"If you give it to another woman, then it won't remind you of my daughter any longer." The mother was growing angry. This man who had driven her daughter mad with longing, who had brought her nothing but despair and then death, seemed to care for nothing but the ring.

"Madame, rest assured, your daughter is with me so long as I have the ring." Gently, he took the mother's hand, turned it palm up and kissed it. She thought she might lose her balance for the tremor his kiss sent through her body. He slipped the ring from her finger and held her hand for a moment in both of his.

Part of her rebuked herself for coveting the ring. But she wanted it. Ever so faintly, she said, "Please, it's all I have left of my daughter."

The man's hazel eyes were like the opal: brilliant, changeable, mercurial. "No, it's all I have left of your daughter," he said and departed.

Outside, Bell slipped the ring on his pinkie and smiled. A perfect fit. He held the opal up to the light. Colors swirled and flamed and faded as if they were engaged in battle with one another. Bell smiled, polished the gemstone with his thumb and said, "I told you we would always be together. Always, my love."

A carriage door opened, and a young woman beckoned to Bell. He entered and sat next to her on the seat. She grabbed his hand, the one with the ring, and squealed with delight.

"Is that it? For me?" she said, awed. The opal glowed in the dim light of the carriage. "The colors are so beautiful." She laughed. "I've never seen anything like it. I swear, the way the colors seem to move, it's like they're trying to leap right out of it."

He laughed, too. "Legend says this is a cursed opal. Those colors, you see? They're souls trapped in there. See that rose color?" he asked pointing to the opal.

She didn't, but she nodded anyway. She wanted Bell to continue flirting. He never flirted, and she was enjoying it.

"That's your soul. The lavender, that's my soul. Take the ring and we're together for eternity."

He slid the ring off of his finger and reached for her hand.

"So the opal's like heaven?"

"Or hell," Bell said and smiled.

"Oh, not hell," the girl said.

She looked at the ring and sighed. "The ring's too big. We'll have to have it sized. Your mother must have large hands."

Bell smiled. "No need." He threaded her slender finger through the ring. "See, it's a perfect fit."

THE PORTRAIT OF JUDGE POTTER

The Kingston Free Library is haunted.

True story. It really is. By a judge who, well, has been known to throw a tantrum or two. The trouble began when they took his portrait down.

The librarians decided that the portrait of Judge William Potter needed some sprucing up. Two hundred years of dust and grime had dulled the judge's dashing visage. And so it was removed from the Kingston Free Library and taken to a restoration shop.

Much to someone's chagrin.

"That's when we noticed more activity," the librarian said. "We figured it was the judge's way of showing he was unhappy with his portrait being removed."

Judge Potter had endowed the library and donated his private book collection to it. If someone were entitled to haunt the Kingston Free Library, certainly that someone was Judge Potter.

And how did the judge show the librarians his displeasure? Did he frighten them? No. He was more of a pest. Well, most felt he was, anyway.

Right: Judge William Potter. *Photo by author*.

Below: Kingston Free Library. *Photo by Kyuss-Apollo*.

Kingston Village, home to a haunted library and one vain ghost. *Photo by author.*

"I never felt frightened," one of the ladies said. "I've always felt that he was benevolent."

"But not everybody feels that way," said another librarian.

"No," the first concurred. "Some feel there's something unpleasant here."

But that could be another ghost entirely. The two ladies talk of a ghost on the second floor, that of a woman. Not everyone likes her, either.

And what of Judge Potter? Have they seen him?

No, they said, but they know he's there.

"On two occasions, I've seen books float off the shelves, drop and land spine upright," said one librarian. "It happened right in front of me."

And on more than one occasion the same librarian found a line of books, single file and upright, in front of the circulation desk where she works. She assumed the night janitor was pulling a prank, but he denied it. What other explanation could there be than that of Judge Potter?

And the man could be impulsive.

Judge Potter gained some unwanted notoriety in his lifetime for building an addition on the abbey, his Kingston home, for an infamous

The Potter family burial plot in Kingston. *Photo by author.*

spiritual leader. The addition was a suite of rooms for the prophetess Jemima Wilkinson, who called herself the "Universal Friend." We will see that her contemporaries may have found double meaning in the title. So Judge Potter had solicited Jemima's help as a miracle worker, another self-appointed title. He had a sickly daughter. Wilkinson's ministrations did no good for the girl. She died of her illness. Wilkinson also ministered to Judge Potter, though the nature of her relations with Judge Potter caused some angst for Mrs. Potter.

Mrs. Potter came upon them one day as Jemima was doing her spiritual work with the judge. The scene must have caused Mrs. Potter some concern, for Jemima found it necessary to say that she was doing the work of God. To which Mrs. Potter famously replied, "Miss Wilkinson, minister to your lambs but leave my old ram alone."

Perhaps the old ram gets a bit randy still when he doesn't have a woman's attentions? Maybe. Especially if he were to think his portrait's removal were permanent.

When Judge Potter's portrait was returned, activity died away. "I think he knows he wasn't forgotten," one librarian said.

It appears so. Books are no longer flying off the shelves.

THE QUEENS OF BELCOURT CASTLE

The candle's flickering light forces us to retreat deeper into our corners. We don't like light. Some of us scurry, but the slow ones are seen. The monk will never live down the photo someone snapped of him skulking around the ladies' room like some kind of Peeping Tom. I prefer voyeur, but that's too elegant a term for someone who spends his afterlife sneaking looks at old ladies using the castle privy.

When the light draws near the knight, we can see him stifle a scream and will himself not to move. Ever since he screamed in front of those girls—how safe we feel in the knowledge that he's guarding us!—we've taken to avoiding him. What an embarrassment. Quaking in his armor like a child. The other suits would move away from him if they could. But they can't. They're tethered to their suits as I am to my chair. We're all here because we're attached to our things. What we coveted most in life becomes our prison in death. The suits of armor can no more move from their dais than I can rise from my throne. Where once we were warriors and monarchs, we are now shadows desperately clinging to what was, unable to stand what is. We are the mummers, the entertainment. How has it come to this?

The wraiths draw nearer to us now. Commoners. They are raucous and loud. Once they would have knelt, paid homage, brought gifts. But now they gape, try to touch things, giggle with their petty insurrections when they succeed. As if striking a key on a piano somehow makes them militant. The more sensitive ones sense they are profane, but they don't grasp why they feel this. They don't understand that they commit a sacrilege. They think what is mine is theirs to touch, and I have to remind them of their place.

Haunted Hallows

The night it happens there is a great group of them. We hear them long before we see them. One of the candle bearers, the one who leads them, is named Alma. She is talking in a low voice, for effect, to make them apprehensive. It's working. Most of the group shies away, gives our chairs a wide berth. Blessed darkness returns as the people—and their candles—retreat. But one woman drifts from the gaggle. Alma does not see her. She is talking about the history of my chair—fifteenth century, intricately carved with cavities for salt, spices and other things of value to a medieval lady of the manor. I snicker. As if a queen would have spices stashed in her throne.

But the moment is short-lived. The woman stretches out her arm. She is going to touch me, and I am horrified. No one touches me. I shrink back into my chair, and the withered hand draws near. Next to me, my lord, as impotent in death as he was in life, presses his body to the back of his chair and slides down. His scant hair stands on end as if from static, but we both know better. Even in my panic I feel disgust. The hand—shaking, spotty, knotted with veins—is inches from my face. What will happen if she touches me? Then I realize she doesn't see me at all. She wants to touch the chair, the throne, and that awakens in me all the old feelings, the fears I held when alive. I worried that I would lose my place. That my husband would see a young girl in his court and resolve to have her. That had been my story, after all, and I had had no illusions that there weren't others with similar agendas.

I feel myself growing hot with anger. Anger at this miserable shadow that is my husband. Anger at this damn chair. And anger that another would dare to touch it. It is all I have left. Then the woman's hand is on my head, and I feel her try to press it down. She would force me down? I wrap my icy fingers around the underside of her wrist and squeeze. She gasps, wriggles her fingers, steps back, but I hold her fast. Now I have her wrist in both hands, and I squeeze as hard as I can as I push her offensive paw up and off my head.

She screams.

Alma, in mid-sentence, stops talking. "What's happening, Mildred?"

"Something has my hand, and I can't get myself free."

I squeeze harder, hoping to break one of the fragile bones beneath the woman's tissue-thin skin. I want her to remember this moment. The woman's eyes bulge, and she begins to shake.

Alma comes to us.

"Don't panic, Mildred. I can help you."

She sees me; I can tell. I try to keep my grip, more out of fear than malice now. Alma comes at me, windmilling and flailing her arms, sweeping her fingers across my head, my hair, my breasts. I let go of the other woman and push Alma's hands away, and as I do, a great ball of light bursts between us. Surely, Alma's a witch. I cower in my chair, tuck my head underneath my arms and hold my palms toward her. Stop, please, just stop.

The one called Mildred swoons. Alma looks ill and totters off toward the exit. The group, three of them propping up Mildred, follows Alma out of the room. When they are gone, there is silence. Shame. I feel it within me and without, and I glare at all in the room, but I say and do nothing. I've proven no better than the cowering knight and perhaps even less regal than my worthless husband. I curl up into my chair and sob.

Sometime later, Alma returns with the queen of the castle.

"They said you went into the ladies' room and stayed there for an hour, Alma."

"Is the woman alright? I am worried about her."

"The woman seemed fine, Alma. In fact, she was more concerned about your welfare than about what had happened to her. She's grateful for your quick thinking. The whole group was anxious to stay to see if you were going to be okay. What in the world happened?"

"I was zapped. I knew what the consequences could be, but I did it anyway. I took the whole jolt."

I rub my cold hands together. In death, you are never warm, but the woman, Alma, was right. In that moment, when my hands broke free from Mildred's wrist and Alma swatted me, I felt a jolt, too. I saw the burst of light. I thought it magic. Alma's magic.

Or was it mine?

I sit up, shoulders back, and look to one side: cowering king. I look to the other: shrinking knight. Fearful. I smile and sit up straight. My magic. My power. I lift one eyebrow, stare at the women. Behold and be awed.

They stay a respectful distance away.

As they should.

THE TREASURE OF CARBUNCLE POND

In the hills of Coventry, where the woods were the thickest and light the faintest, there lived a serpent. It was no ordinary snake. It was huge—a beast with fangs the length of a grown man's arm and a mouth large enough to take a bull in two gulps. It was the most fearsome thing in the countryside, and if there were any doubt as to the serpent's supremacy over man and beast, the pulsing carbuncle atop its head seemed a clear sign of its being anointed by the devil himself.

It was greed for the carbuncle, a jewel the size of a plate, that drove the natives to hunt the beast and to wage war with one another. But the people did not look upon the gem as something to be worn but rather something to be wielded. The few who'd seen the snake and lived to tell of it believed the stone could alert its bearer of the presence of prey and predator both.

According to the elders, the snake's carbuncle, usually translucent, glowed a deep, ruby red when it hunted and an emerald green when danger neared. The tribe that had such a treasure would surely be invincible. And so it was that many young braves with dreams of greatness disappeared in those woods on what would become known as Carbuncle Hill.

The tribe grew weak for lack of young men, so it was decided that a group of the fiercest remaining warriors would enter the forest and kill the snake. They'd bait a trap for the serpent. They'd place a boy in his path, an orphan child who would not be missed if he were to be taken. Most of the tribe did not even know his name, calling him "boy" or "you" when they wanted him. Nor did they know his face, for he kept his head bowed and his voice low as a whisper. He was slow, they reasoned.

His death would be no loss. It was decided. While the serpent was busy with the boy, they would attack.

The boy was not slow, either of mind or foot. He was willing, though, to do this for his tribe. Whether he lived or died was unimportant; either way, he would be a hero. To live as an outcast was a far worse fate. And so he entered the forest one evening and ran toward the crimson light that glowed there. He could hear the beast tear through the woods, knocking down trees and sending rocks ricocheting in his haste to taste human flesh. It seemed only moments until the two met at opposite ends of Carbuncle Pond. The boy entered the water, closing the distance between himself and the snake. The snake's eyes glowed red like the carbuncle as its head reared up, poised to take the boy with one snap of its jaws. It was then that the hidden warriors released dozens of flaming, poisoned arrows into the mouth of the beast. The snake flailed, mouth agape as flames filled its throat. As it fell, it opened its mouth still wider and took the boy as it plunged headfirst into the water.

The warriors wailed not for the loss of the boy but for the jewel. And in their misery, they did not immediately see the boy rise out of the water, jewel in one hand and dagger in the other.

"I have it," he said, holding up the carbuncle, which was, once again, translucent.

The warriors rejoiced—for a moment. Then they fell to fighting over whose arrow had killed the beast and who deserved to bring the treasure back to the tribe. The boy's words stopped their fighting, so surprised were they to hear him talk.

"The stone will choose its master," he said, holding the jewel in his outstretched hand.

The warriors pushed and shoved one another in their haste to claim the stone. But when they touched it, it burned their hands with a heat so fierce it blistered their palms. One by one they grabbed the stone. One by one they threw themselves into the pond, seeking the balm of cool water upon their singed hands. When all were prostrate, the boy spoke again.

"It is the stone's will that I be its caretaker," the boy said. "With it, I shall know where game grazes and danger hides. If you want the stone's gifts, you must accept its master."

The warriors agreed to the boy's demands, thinking to take the carbuncle from him later, but he placed the rock in a leather pouch and sewed it to the skin of his chest. "As the carbuncle acted as a third eye for the serpent, so it will do for me."

The boy became the tribe's shaman and reaped the rewards of a hero. He married the sachem's daughter and was given a place of honor in the tribe. He was blessed with many children and for many years brought prosperity to his people. They had all the game they could eat, and no enemy could draw near without notice.

It was with the arrival of the white men that things began to change. They, too, had heard tales of the carbuncle, and, as the natives had done before them, the colonists planned to take the stone from its bearer. As before, an ambush was planned, and the shaman found himself at Carbuncle Pond, this time face to face with a white man and his gun. This time, the shaman's knife failed him. The bullet entered the shaman's belly, and he felt as if he had swallowed a thousand flaming arrows.

In his last moments of life, the shaman ripped the carbuncle from his chest and lobbed it into the air. All around him he could hear the cries of horror—from his tribesmen and the white warriors. The carbuncle flashed green and then red before dropping into the pond. And as it sank, so did the shaman, alone and forgotten once more as the natives and the white men waded toward the spot where the carbuncle had descended. There was more bloodshed, more death, but no one was able to recover the stone.

The few who survived that night said the shaman placed a spell on the stone to keep it translucent and invisible. Others said it hadn't fallen into the water at all but rather rose to the heavens, where it became a star. But there are a few who believe the jewel sits on the bottom of Carbuncle Pond, waiting to choose its next master.

And so it may remain, waiting for another who is worthy.

TUGGIE BANNOCKS AND THE WITCH SHEEP

Tuggie Bannocks was sure, dead sure, that old Mum Amey was witch-riding her at night. She'd wake with a sore back, dirt caked under her fingernails and an ache in her jaw, as if it had been stretched taut by a bit. And now Tuggie's waking hours weren't offering her any protection, either.

Tuggie was scared—so scared that to think on it too long set her bones shaking and her teeth chattering. Old Mum Amey was an older, meaner and more powerful witch than Tuggie, and Old Mum Amey was growing bolder.

A wet and wild-eyed Tuggie burst into Benny and Debby Nichols's Narragansett home one night after Christmas. With the wind gusting behind her, the old woman's raggedy clothes billowed and undulated; she looked like a wraith and howled like a banshee, and the Nicholses cowered at the sight of her. Benny Nichols nearly dropped his mug of flip, he was so startled. Tuggie threw herself facedown on the Nicholses' table—no one had ever seen her sit in a chair—and told Benny to give her his mug of beer. "And don't you go lightly on the Jamaica rum and sugar, Benny Nichols," she warned. "I be needin' it."

Debby took the sodden, woolen shawl from Tuggie's shoulders and murmured her disapproval of Tuggie's traipsing about in snow with only rags tied to her feet. Benny was up and fixing Tuggie's brew as fast as he could. Beer, rum and sugar—all in generous quantities—were set by Tuggie's reclining head. She did not thank Benny but glowered at him instead.

"Not bubbling? That ain't near hot enough, Benny."

"Sorry, Miz Tuggie," Benny said. He took the hot poker from the fire and put it in the mug until the liquid bubbled and steam rose. Then he returned the mug to Tuggie.

"Better," she said and nodded at Benny. She turned to her side, propped her head up with one hand and used the other to serve herself. Debby brought her a plate of venison stew and some bread. She undid the rags from the old woman's feet and took a basket of broken eggs from her arm. Tuggie patted Debby's arm.

"Thank you, Missus. You'll dry my stockings by your fire, won't you?"

"Yes, Miss Tuggie," Debby said, "but I'm afraid I can't do much about your eggs. They mashed to bits."

When Tuggie had eaten and drunk her fill, she rose from the table. A freed slave, she was tall and gaunt with two full rows of double teeth. Her face was bronze, shrunken and wrinkled like a dried apple, and her hands were so bony that the fingers looked more like talons. Tiny pigtails of gray hair had escaped the scarlet turban she always wore. Benny and Debby knew something must have scared her good to put her out of order. Miss Tuggie prided herself on her appearance, often saying she was the last of a long line of powerful voodoo priestesses, a daughter of Queen Abigail herself.

Though she was old, Tuggie was strong. She never stood still when she visited the Nicholses, despite their repeated invitations to sit a spell. Someone so old must surely be tired. But she never seemed so. Tonight, she paced back and forth in front of the hearth. It made Bennie nervous to watch her pacing and muttering like she did. He worried she was spell-casting. But he said nothing. You don't question a witch.

People said Tuggie did not have a single chair in her house because she preferred to hang by her heels like a bat from the wainscoting in her kitchen. Chepa Rose swore Tuggie was a witch, said he saw her run round the room on just the molding one night. Schoolchildren thought so, too. They'd jeer at her and yell, "Te-Rap, Te-Rap!" because, the older ones told the younger, that was how witches greeted one another.

And old Tuggie really didn't mind people thinking she was a witch. She was a prideful woman, and she liked people fearing her. She also liked the money they'd pay for a love potion or a hex or a blessing on their fields. It was a lot easier work than washing and carding wool or stirring soap for hours on end. Debby Nichols always enlisted Tuggie's help in soap-making and told people it was the voodoo charms she muttered that made her soap the finest in Narragansett. Tuggie liked that about Debby.

Benny was scared of Tuggie, and she liked that, too.

If you crossed her, Tuggie knew how to make you sorry. With flour, water, a few hairs from your head and a couple of pins, she could give you hobblin' rheumatism. With a pair of rusty nails, the tail of a smoked herring, a handful of Narragansett graveyard dirt, a rabbit's foot and something of yours, she could brew up a potion that would have you sick before it started bubbling.

Tonight, Tuggie wore her skirts inside out and a string of eggshells around her neck. The smell of rotten egg hung heavy in the hot air. Debby knew Tuggie's ways. These were charms to ward off devils.

"Miz Tuggie, what have you been up to?"

"Ye know, Missus, I told ye I was witch-rid by old Mum Amey, and this is how I knew: I had had the dreams. Her sitting on me and drawin' the breath from my body. I feared I would die! I was just going to work a project, a charm on her first off—not to hurt her none, jess bother her a little."

Miss Tuggie checked Debby's reaction to this. Debby nodded.

"Well, she knowed, somehow, what I was doing. She appeared in my kitchen one day, walked over to the chimney to light her pipe and asked me what I was cookin'. And I said I was making glue."

"Had you put the rabbit's foot in the pot yet?" Debby asked. Debby knew the witch's most important ingredient in any spell was the rabbit's foot.

"No. I took the pot off the crane; I didn't want her lookin' in," Tuggie said. "But Mum Amey just laughed and told me glue would never hold her fast. 'No spell of yours, Tuggie, will touch me,'" she said.

The hagging got much, much worse. "Mornings when I wake, I see marks on my mouth where Mum Amey has been draining me. And my hands and feet! They're cut to ribbons." Tuggie showed Debby the palms of her hands. They were red and oozing. She's been riding me—all over Boston Neck and up Ridge Hill till I'm so tired I drop. I wake up and I can't move!"

Mum Amey was pulling her hair and pinching her, too. She showed Debby and Benny the purple and black bruises on her neck and shoulders. "I'd show you what her scabby heels had done to my flanks, but it wouldn't be proper with him in the room," Tuggie said, tilting her head at Benny. He flushed red and looked down.

"And my butter wouldn't come out right till I dropped a red-hot horseshoe into the cream to drive her out."

"But how do you know Mum Amey is doing these things? How do you know you didn't make the glue wrong or the butter?" Benny asked. Tuggie glared at him and growled. "I wasn't makin' glue, and I knowed what I was doin'."

Tuggie addressed Debby.

"She talks to animals. That black cat that follows her. The one she calls Coal. She talks to it. And when she thinks no one sees her, she pricks her finger and nurses it with her blood."

Debby Nichols gasped and crossed herself.

"I had a silver coin, one you gave me, Missus," Tuggie said. "I dropped it at my door when she warn't looking and invited her in. She smiled at me and shook her head. Witches won't step over silver. They won't."

"And now," Tuggie paused and peered into the shadowy areas in Debby Nichols's small kitchen, inclining her head left and then right, looking down at the floor and up to the ceiling. "Now, she's shifting."

"Shifting?" Benny Nichols raised an eyebrow.

"Shifting," Tuggie said and nodded. "She's changing. From witch to sheep and back again."

"No," Debby said. "God help us. How will we know her if she comes?"

"I don't believe it," Benny said, but he didn't sound so sure of himself.

"I know, Benny Nichols. I know for sure she's a witch. I seen her just now in the moonlight chasin' and ridin' your sheep. And, sure as you were born, you'll find some of them stone dead in the morning—all of 'em, maybe!"

"How will we know her if she's a sheep?" Debby asked.

"Oh, she's monstrous, a fearsome thing to see," Tuggie said, eyes wide. "Witches don't never go about in their own form when they go to Sabbath. Old Mum Amey, she was long and low, like a snake. She ran along the ground, wooly and white in the moonlight, jumpin' and leapin' and springin' at them poor sheep—and them bleating their terrors!"

"But how do you know it's her? For sure?" Benny asked.

"She be wearing her bedding—a red and blue blanket tied up around her belly. And there are gold dollars dottin' her back—payment from the

A bewitching sheep. *Photo by George Gastin.*

devil, I expect, for her evil-doin'. Sometimes she jumps in the air and spreads her demon wings, and smoke and sparks come out of her mouth and nostrils. And the horns! She's got black horns sproutin' from her head. And a tail, like she's the very devil, himself."

"Oh, God," cried Debby. "The devil's outside."

Benny had a different reaction. He laughed. Quietly at first and then heartily. Tuggie scowled.

"Oh, Miz Tuggie, I have good news. There's no devil in my fields. And no Mum Amey, either. Your witch is an old ewe of mine who got caught in a snowdrift. It took me a few days to find her, and when I finally did, I found she'd eaten her own coat right off!"

Tuggie was not amused or relieved.

"You dare laugh at me, Benny Nichols?"

Benny struggled to control himself.

"Oh, Miss Tuggie, I mean no harm. I'm just relieved is all. She's just an ewe. She's no witch. Debby, tell her. Tell her it's my old coat with the brass buttons the sheep's wearing."

Debby nodded. "It's true, Miss Tuggie. I put the coat on her myself."

Tuggie drew her coat around her shoulders and grabbed the rags Debby had set to dry by the stove. She wrapped them around her feet and waved away Benny's peace offering of more flip. "High time you stopped such outrageous goin's-on—dressin' up sheep like devils—scarin' an old woman to death an breaking all her eggs. Old Tuggie Bannocks ain't forgotten how to burn a project. I know many charms." She drew close to Benny and pointed a hoary finger at his chest. "Guess you won't laugh at a witch then."

Debby tried to make peace with the old woman, but she wouldn't be moved. She gathered up her dripping eggs, her wet rags and her injured pride and returned to the night. On her way home, she kicked the witch sheep in the rump, sending it into another snowdrift.

"Go on, then, eat your coat and choke on your buttons," she yelled at the bleating ewe.

When she entered her own little hovel half an hour later, the fire was nearly out. Just a few embers kept the room from total darkness, so she did not see the hunched figure in the corner until she'd fed the fire with the few remaining logs by the hearth.

"You shouldn't kick an innocent creature. Or an old witch, Tuggie Bannocks," Old Mum Amey said, smiling widely, showing off her own double set of teeth.

Tuggie shrank at the site of Old Mum Amey in her red and blue coat with the brass buttons.

"Now, to the knees with you," the old witch said. "We have miles to go before the night's through."

When Benny Nichols ventured out to tend to his flock the next morning, he found his old witch sheep stuck in a drift once more. He grabbed the shivering thing by her hindquarters and freed her, laughing again at Tuggie's foolishness. But he didn't laugh for long. Tuggie made good on her threats. On windy nights, Debby and Benny would hear her alight on their roof, scrambling about as if she were on her hands and knees. She'd blow ash and soot down their chimney, and above the screeching winds they would hear her muffled cries, "Curse you, Benny Nichols. You are no Christian man. You and Old Mum Amey! You do the devil's work!"

All that winter, poor Debby Nichols's cakes burnt in the fire, and her charred roasts fell from the spit. And all of Debby's petticoats bore singe marks, even though she wore them inside out. Benny grew wan and thin with worry and lack of proper nourishment. The Nicholses might have suffered indefinitely if not for the fortunate appearance of a wolf that, one fine spring evening, caught the witch sheep by the throat and made a fine meal of her before being shot by Benny. Later, he heard that Old Mum Amey had died the same hour from injuries brought about by violent fits. The doctor who examined Old Mum Amey said that the woman had torn her own throat apart.

Tuggie Bannocks must have had a change of heart with the witch sheep's death because her haunting of the Nicholses stopped. Finally, Debby was able to feed her husband something other than ash. So happy were the Nicholses with their change of fortune that they spread the story of their witching far and wide so that every farmer, wife and child from Point Judith to Pottawomut knew Tuggie Bannocks to be the most fearsome witch in Washington County. And the Nicholses' flock came to be known throughout Narragansett as witch sheep.

HOW MARK DODGE STILLED THE DANCING MORTAR

In those days on Block Island, when the witch Dutch Kattern trolled its lonely shores and the madman Mark Dodge set the windmill ablaze, when pirates buried pots of gold beneath their murdered mates and the ghost ship *Palatine* set the horizon aflame, there was a haunted house.

Old-fashioned pestle and mortar. *Photo by Vassil.*

And in that house was a very unusual bowl.

It was a wooden mortar, hewn from one of the lignum vitae logs of the *Palatine* that had washed ashore after the ship burned and the wreckers looted what they could. The mortar, like the beleaguered survivors of the *Palatine*, found its way to the home of Simon Ray. Maybe it was one of the survivors who carved it from the salvaged timber—a thank-you gift for Simon Ray's offering of food and shelter.

It was an impressive basin, big enough to bathe a baby, and very heavy. But its size was the only remarkable thing about it, while Simon Ray and his kin were alive anyway.

But when the family passed and madman Mark Dodge moved into the Ray home, strange things began to happen. Of course, Dodge was not

Shipwreck off Block Island. *Postcard from author's collection.*

View of Block Island. *Photo by James Manni.*

the most reliable witness. He said he shared the home with spirits. And he and the witch Kattern were known opium eaters. She said she left her body to pay visits to family in Europe. He set fires.

With the Ray family's house came its contents, so the mortar came to be in the possession of Mark Dodge. But he said it had become possessed. Of its own accord, it began to shake and then threw itself on its side in order to spin and roll around the room. Then it righted itself and hopped as high as the rafters. Terrified, Mark Dodge opened his doors and drove the bedeviled mortar from his home. He took an axe to it but could not cleave spirit from matter. Finally, he took boulders from a stone wall and tethered the mortar beneath them, stopping its dancing once and for all.

THE MOANING BONES OF MOUNT TOM

In the deep woods of Arcadia, nestled amid the white ash and black birch, there once was a little farm at the base of Mount Tom. In the shadow of its granite cliffs lived a farmer and his daughter. Early one evening, a lone peddler knocked on the door and asked if he might have food and a place to sleep for the night. The Mount Tom Trail was a lonely stretch of road. The Rathbun house, a cemetery and a cattle pound were the only evidence of civilization. As the dark descended and the dense forest shadows grew, the light from the little farmhouse must have seemed a beacon to the weary man.

The peddler said that he would sharpen every knife in the place in exchange for the farmer's hospitality. The farmer agreed, and the three sat down to dinner. After the meal, the daughter cleared, cleaned, bid the peddler good night and retired to her upstairs bedroom. The peddler had already begun sharpening the few knives in the farmer's possession. Sometime later, the girl was awoken by a scuffle below. Fearing for her father, she grabbed her robe and flew down the stairs. There was her father, standing over the still body of the peddler. Toppled furniture, the peddler's bag and silver were scattered across the farmhouse floor. The farmer had a newly sharpened, newly bloodied knife in hand.

The girl fell to floor, pawing through the peddler's wares, her avarice overriding any horror she might have felt at her father's actions. The girl's greed, though, was not enough to convince her father that she would keep his secret. With the same bloody knife he'd used to slit the peddler's throat, he sawed off his daughter's tongue.

Years passed, and the father and daughter died. The house stayed empty, and over time, nature took up residence—blackberry vines, weeds and water consuming the clapboard until all that remained was the foundation and the hearth. In time, more people came to live at the base of Mount Tom, and their children played among the farmhouse ruins. That is, until the day the hearth moaned.

Terrified, the children ran to their parents, who returned with picks and shovels to dismantle the hearth. And there, among the dirt and dust, lay the bones of the poor peddler.

ANOTHER TALE OF A RESTLESS SPIRIT WITH AN AXE TO GRIND

Find that last story farfetched? If only. Variations on the murdered-moaning-guy-buried-in-the-basement story are somewhat commonplace in Rhode Island. It's a little distressing to think that many of our early stonemasons were perfecting their craft while walling up their murder victims, certainly. Then again, Edgar Allan Poe must have gotten the idea for the "Cask of Amontillado" from somewhere, right? Maybe Narragansett, for instance.

On Narragansett's old Indian Trail lies the foundation of another long-abandoned house. It was once the home of a mean and miserly old man and his son. Neighbors told stories to one another about how the man beat his boy. Some whispered that it wasn't enough for the old man to use his fists on his son. No, the old bastard used the head of an axe.

Then one day, the boy was just gone. His father said he'd run off to sea, but there were those who believed he'd finally beaten the boy to death. Those who held to this theory believed the boy's remains to be in the basement. The cruel man was not brought before any court, but judgment was passed, nonetheless. When the old man died, no one mourned his loss, and there was none who wanted to keep vigil the night before his burial. One Kingston man finally relented and agreed to sit by the body that night. For a while, the evening passed uneventfully. The man even dozed off for a time.

He was awakened by a noise. The front door had been unlatched and was opened to the outdoors. The man closed the door and settled back in his spot by the corpse. Not long afterward, the man witnessed the door unlatch itself. He arose and latched the door a second time. Again, the man witnessed the door unlatch itself and swing open.

Not easily spooked and extraordinarily handy, the man whittled a wooden plug and attempted to jam the latch closed. Unseen hands were unaffected by the deterrent. The plug popped like a cork, and the house was again open to the dark night. Before the man could rise again to close the door, a heavy object flew through the air and landed on the floor of the room. It was an axe head. Evidence of an unsolved murder or a morbid prank? The man did not know. He just shut the door once more. And this time, it stayed shut.

THE ONE WHO GOT AWAY?

This story begins in Egypt with an ancient curse—a dark, winged thing that traveled through time and across oceans to find the men who had awakened her. From the dust, she'd risen—hot, angry and thirsty for the blood of the infidels, commoners who'd hollowed out the Valley of the Kings like ants with no nobler aims than grave robbers. They'd broken into the pharaohs' tombs, trampling sacred hallows in their zeal to steal the very gods and goddesses themselves from their beds.

This story ends in Coconut Grove, Miami, at Villa Serena, the home of Secretary of State William Jennings Bryan. Here, on February 23, 1915, Egyptologist Theodore M. Davis, age seventy-eight, began his own journey into the afterlife. Ten years earlier, Davis had been credited with the greatest discovery ever unearthed at the Valley of the Kings at Thebes: the discovery of the tombs of Queen Teie's parents. Queen Teie was the favorite wife of Amen-hotep, the heretic king. And this find would lead to other discoveries: of the tombs of Amen-hotep, Rameses IX and, still later, King Tutankhamen. But in their discovery, many believe something was released. Something vengeful appeased only by death.

The Curse watched as the tomb raiders justified their looting with the promise that the antiquities they'd discovered were destined for museums—after their deaths, of course. After they'd enjoyed and even been honored for their plundering. They said the world had a right to see and to learn the secrets of the kings. They wanted to exhibit and to study the holy treasures. And the world was receptive, even appreciative.

The Curse no doubt marveled at their insolence. These wretched creatures believed they had the right to pick and paw at ancient kings, their queens and their belongings without fear of retribution? They dared to pack their bodies in crates, destined for display like some traveling circus?

In their greed for money and glory, they'd ignored the warning. Her warning: "Cursed be those who disturb the rest of a pharaoh. They that shall break the seal of this tomb shall meet death by a disease that no doctor can diagnose."

Did the men find it charmingly anachronistic? A tantalizing postscript to their tales of adventure shared with guests as they conducted tours of their own temples—grand homes built from the profits they'd reaped and filled with pharaohs' treasures. Did they suffer any guilt at having taken the priceless gold and jewels meant to guarantee those ancient kings safe passage to the afterlife? Some, perhaps.

But did Davis?

His grand Newport home, the Reef, was a seaside American castle of shingle and stone, the jewel of Brenton Point. Here, Davis displayed his extensive collection of Egyptian antiquities amassed during expeditions he'd commissioned in 1889 and 1912. One of his prized possessions was an alabaster reproduction of Queen Teie's head: "I always keep that portrait as a memento of a very beautiful and attractive lady whom I am sorry I did not have the opportunity of meeting."

What must the gods have thought of such arrogance? Queen Teie, the kept woman of an infidel? What price would Davis pay for such a crime?

Because people did pay. Dearly.

Some saw the Curse coming and were afraid. Desperate to escape her, they sought the help of physicians and, when those failed, magicians. But

The Valley of the Kings, Thebes. *Photo by Haloorange.*

Another view of the Valley of the Kings. *Photo by Nowic.*

the Curse would not be kept at bay. One by one, she took the men who had dared to trespass in the Valley of the Kings.

Lord Carnarvon she slew with a lowly mosquito; for his half brother, she chose blood poisoning. To George J. Gould, she sent a fever. To Howard Carter, cancer. Prince Ali and Woolf Joel she felled with bullets. To A.C. Mace, she fed arsenic. Bethell the elder, she pushed. Bethell the younger, she smothered. And it went on.

But no such drama surrounded Davis's death. In fact, the *New York Times* article said only that he died. And it was ten years after his great discovery. Wouldn't a curse work faster than that?

Perhaps. Then again, maybe the Curse was clever.

Davis died far from the Reef and his prized possessions. He was deprived of a last look at his treasures. The serene face of Queen Teie, his memento, was far from view at the moment of his death. As he deprived her of her final resting place, so, too, was he cheated. But did the Curse do him one better? The Valley of the Kings remains; the Reef was consumed by fire in 1961. Queen Teie is remembered. Davis is forgotten.

A TALE OF NINE MEN'S MISERY

In March 1676, nine men met a brutal death on a battlefield in Cumberland.

It was early spring, the Lord's Day, when a band of eighty or so East Providence men set off for Central Falls with the intention of killing the Narragansetts encamped there. It was traditionally a day of rest for Christians, but those early settlers probably believed their actions were justified, given their absolute conviction that all native people were at best heathens or at worst demons, Satan's servants. So what better employment for God-fearing men than cold-blooded killing on a brisk Sunday morning?

The colonial war party sent a messenger to Providence asking that the men there join it in its endeavor. The messenger arrived during services, though, and, being a good Christian, was loathe to deliver his message until worship ended.

So he waited.

For four hours.

When the Providence reinforcements finally arrived, they saw a grisly sight: seventy bloody corpses strewn about. Evidently, God was not on the side of the colonists that day.

Ten men were unaccounted for. Nine were eventually found. There was evidence that they'd been tortured. They'd also been decapitated. The nine headless men were mourned and then buried in a common grave in Cumberland under a cairn. In 1928, a permanent marker was installed on the site. It bears a plaque on which the following is inscribed: "On this spot, where they were slain by the Indians, were buried the nine soldiers captured in Pierce's Fight, March 26, 1676."

Nothing is known of what became of the tenth man.

But the skulls turned up.

In the 1960s, a man named Joseph K. Ott, a volunteer for the Rhode Island Historical Society, found a carton in the basement of the society's headquarters. In the carton were bones and nine skulls with a card identifying the contents as the remains of "Nine Men's Misery."

Not your usual day at the office.

THE LAST VOYAGE OF THE *SEABIRD*

Late in the night, long after the men had left the tavern, long after their wives had fallen asleep beside them, only then in the dark and silence did they let loose their fear. Exhausted, they flinched at every crack and creak that echoed through their homes. What had come ashore that morning? What might be wandering out there, in the dark, right now?

For no ship can sail without a captain and crew.

But one did.

It was 1750, Newport, at the eastern end of Easton's Beach, by the road to Purgatory and Second Beach. Farmers and fishermen were the first to see the vessel and wonder at why it seemed intent on wrecking itself.

From out of nowhere, the *Seabird* appeared. "All sails set and her colors flying," one of the fishermen said to everyone and no one in particular. People who lived on the Newport shore had joined the other witnesses. Women began to worry aloud about what would happen. The water was rough that morning and the coast rocky.

Even more disturbing: there was no crew to be seen on the ship's deck. The coastline's crags and ledges had made driftwood of many vessels, but this one skirted its gaping maw effortlessly. Only the most skilled crew could manage such a thing, and only in an emergency. But this ship chose to place itself in harm's way.

When the *Seabird*'s unmolested keel struck sand, the crowd made an audible sound of relief. The children in the group ran to the ship. The mothers ran faster, grabbing their children and pulling them back, sensing something sinister. For there were still no signs of life aboard the ship.

The young men in the crowd, those wanting to boast of their bravado, were the first to board the ship.

What they reported caused some to cross themselves and whisper prayers. What fools they had been to come to this foreign land! A place of devils, demons, witches, monsters—and ghost ships.

The only crew left aboard was a dog on deck and a cat in the cabin. Coffee was boiling on the galley stove. And breakfast had been prepared. Nothing was upended or strewn about. It was if someone had just ducked down below for a moment.

But a search of the entire ship turned up not another living thing.

One man noted that the ship's longboat was missing. Clearly, he said, the crew abandoned ship, probably when the ship headed for the breakers.

But no other vessel had come into view, and in the days that followed, there were no reports of a crew coming ashore, dead or alive.

What little that could be learned was this: The *Seabird* was the property of a Newport merchant and under the command of a Captain John Huxham. He and his crew were expected in Newport after a voyage to Honduras. But neither Huxham nor his crew were ever heard from again.

In another time and place, the *Seabird* might have been decommissioned or destroyed. But this was eighteenth-century America. Ghost boat or not, no self-respecting colonist was going to dispose of a perfectly good vessel. Hell, the thing sailed itself. But it would be the *Seabird* no longer.

The Newport merchant sold his cursed ship to a new owner, who changed its name to the *Beach Bird*. No further incidents of crews vanishing were reported.

Part II

Monsters' Lairs

A VISIT TO THE SHUNNED HOUSE

My mother would pick up her pace and tug on my hand as we passed the yellow house at 135 Benefit Street. I would slow my step, dragging the toes of my sneakers across the sidewalk. It was such a pretty, pretty house.

I couldn't understand why my mother wouldn't want to idle there, to peer over the yellow picket fence and admire the yellow and red tulips that swayed in the breeze like lithe ballerinas, blondes and redheads wearing green blouses that billowed at the sleeves. I would try to peer in between the slats of the home's two shuttered, basement-level doors. The basement was partially above ground, and I was a curious child. But when I grew older and bolder and my mother a bit slower, I found that the home's sunny façade kept its contents to itself. Nothing ever stirred its curtains. No one even ever stepped out to shoo me away.

I imagined the house was home to a lovely old woman, a master gardener, a cookie baker, perhaps a painter, too. Someone who saw the magic in everyday things. Like me.

My mom didn't see the same things.

"It's a graveyard dressed up as a garden," she spat and crossed herself as she did. We were Catholic. This was common behavior for my mother. "The devil's greatest trick, you know, is making people think he doesn't exist."

The Shunned House, Providence. *Photo by author.*

I sighed but didn't argue. I didn't understand how my mother could see the devil in such a beautiful house. And she wouldn't elaborate. She always gave me the same non-answer when she didn't want to answer my questions. "Be careful what you let into your head," she would say. "Once it's there, you can't get it back out."

When I was old enough to ramble about College Hill on my own, I would make regular visits to the Providence Athenaeum. It was there that I first heard the story of the Shunned House.

The librarian handed me a book, the complete works of Providence author H.P. Lovecraft. He was a strange-looking man. His face appeared pulled, like you might do to an image reproduced on Silly Putty. From his picture, I couldn't tell how old he was or whether he was happy being an author. I always thought I'd grin from ear to ear if I knew my picture would be placed on a book I'd written. Lovecraft, though, seemed miffed, peeved, pissed off.

"He wasn't a happy guy," the young librarian told me. She was pale and wistful with a sad smile. I thought Lovecraft and she would make a good pair. "I think he was tormented."

The Providence Athenaeum, Providence. *Photo by author.*

"By bullies?"

"Demons."

I wasn't sure I believed in demons and said so.

"Oh, I'm not saying I do, either," the librarian said. "But he liked to write about monsters—slimy, crawly, nasty creatures that slunk out of the shadows and drove you mad with fright. He also liked to walk late at night around Providence, and I wonder if he didn't imagine seeing such things.

"You know, an overactive imagination can be dangerous," she said.

"My mother says that, too."

"Well, she's right," said the librarian and nodded her head. "But if you still want to know about the Shunned House, read the story. Lovecraft made it famous."

I did—by flashlight, under my bedcovers, after everyone else had fallen asleep. My father often wondered what pleasure I got from "scaring myself silly," as he put it, and truthfully, I couldn't answer him. I just couldn't help myself.

The Story of the Shunned House in 137 Words

A boy and his uncle decide to spend the night in the basement of the house to find out what evil lives there. They suspect it's a vampire brought here by the French, specifically a family of witches or werewolves. All the people who live in the house either die or go insane (not sure who's luckier). One woman rants about something picking at her like she's a Thanksgiving turkey or something.

The boy and the man encounter some kind of misty, yellowy, tendrilly thing that rises up from the dirt floor of the basement. The uncle starts rolling around speaking French before turning into a monster and melting. The boy, though, survives and eventually kills the evil thing by pouring acid on it. Like it's mold or something. Like, death by bleach. Ick.

I brought the book back to the library. The anemic librarian was there again.

"So, what did you think?"

"It wasn't very scary. Just icky. Lots of mold and glowy stuff, and then the uncle goes crazy, and the kid pours acid on a blob and that's it? Over? Kinda boring."

The librarian smiled. It was the kind of smile someone gives you when you're not in on the joke. Or when you've said something that the adult thinks shows your age and immaturity. I hated that kind of smile.

"Oh, I don't know about that," she said. "Aren't stories the scariest when the monster stays hidden? Or when the monster's right there in plain sight but the character's too dense to see it? I think those are the scariest stories—when the monster's right in front of you all along."

"Well, yeah, but I like the stories where you get to see the monster get his— or hers. I like it when there's a big fight scene and the hero takes it down."

"But that doesn't really happen that often in true horror. Or real life, for that matter," the librarian said. She'd taken the Lovecraft book in hand and was tracing the lines of the author's face with her finger.

"What do you mean?"

"Well, especially in the movies. Most of the time the hero only thinks he's killed the monster, but the audience knows it's still alive. And think about how many times criminals are released from jail to do the same crimes again. Again. And again."

She studied me. I felt uncomfortable in front of her. Not scared but weird, like she was considering me. Would I be the type to kill or be killed? Up until that moment, I was pretty sure I'd be the hero in a horror story. I was smart, bookish and brunette and not too good at sports. Killers always went for the pretty cheerleaders and the football players. At least at first.

"Hmm," the librarian said, placing the book on her cart. "So, can I help you with anything else?"

It was growing late, and I was the last one in the library that Saturday. I had a thought and inadvertently said it aloud. I was annoyed with her and her superiority. I felt I had something to prove.

"I'm going to ring the doorbell of the Shunned House and ask to see the basement on my way home tonight."

"Are you?" the librarian asked and laughed. "Seriously, I wouldn't do that. The owners have that sign about a guard dog. You could get hurt."

"I've never seen a dog."

"Doesn't mean there's not one."

"Well, I'll take my chances."

"You may get yelled at. I'm sure the poor people who own that house are bothered all hours of the day and night. Even if there's no dog, that sign's there for a reason."

"Well, if I get yelled at, so what? I'm not scared."

"That house scares me. I cross the street rather than walk by that house," the librarian said. She was up and turning off lights. "Well, you're not my child, so you don't have to listen to me, but I feel obligated to tell you to stay away. I wouldn't want your mother to think I was the one putting those thoughts in your head."

It was twilight when I left the library. I was determined I would ring the doorbell of the Shunned House on my way home. I jogged there. I had to be home before it got too dark. The house looked beautiful in the sunset—golden with a wash of rose from the pinkening sky. I ran up the stone steps, past the tiny white tin signs. The first: ATTENTION CHIEN BIZARRE. The second: CHIEN FORT MECHANT ET PEU NOURRI. The third: CHIEN LUNATIQUE. The last: DUBLIEZ LE CHIEN ATTENTION AU MAITRE.

I didn't speak or read French. But *lunatique* I got. Still, I was so close.

I opened the gate and ran up the steps, past the tulips, up to the green door. I knocked. I stood and waited as twilight crept up College Hill, casting shadows all around. I lost my nerve. I started to turn.

And the door opened.

Just as I expected, a kind-faced, white-haired woman was at the door. She wore a long dress, old-fashioned but pretty. She had a bunch of tulips on her arm and gardening sheers. She must have just been outdoors herself. I could smell something cinnamony—snickerdoodles, maybe?—coming up the hallway.

"Ah," she said, looking down at me and smiling. "I can guess why you've come."

"Excuse me? I just wanted…"

"You wanted to see the house, the basement, to see where it happened."

"Um, well, yes." This was too easy. "I wanted to see…wait. Where it happened?" Did she mean where the story was written?

She looked puzzled.

"Where they killed the monster, right? Isn't that why you're here?"

"Well, I read the story," I said.

"Yes. The account. And you want to see where it happened," she insisted. She stepped back. "Come in. I'll take you down there."

I bit my lip and shivered. The air was cooling, and the sun had dropped from view. Did I want to go down there? It was why I'd come. I'd be the only kid in school to have seen the Shunned House from the inside. Popularity was within my reach.

The old lady stepped aside, waving me in with her armful of tulips. You could trust a gardener, right? People who grew such beautiful plants had to be good—well, except in that Hawthorne story we'd read in English class: "Rappaccini's Daughter." And *Little Shop of Horrors*. But this was just some ordinary little old lady in Providence who baked cookies and was willing to let a curious kid have a look at her house.

Still.

I stalled for time.

"So, did Lovecraft go down there? That's what you mean when you say, 'Where it happened.'"

"Who? No, I mean that's where it happened. That's where they found him and killed him." She clumsily crossed herself, hard to do with tulips and shears. "Dieu merci."

I stepped back. Of course, there were no vampires in the basement, but crazy ladies with sharp gardening tools could be pretty dangerous, too.

"I would, but it's getting dark, and my mom will be expecting me."

The woman tilted her head and looked at me quizzically.

"But aren't you curious?"

I'd hopped down the steps. Backward. For some reason, I thought it was important that I not turn my back on her. Those gardening sheers again.

"No, I don't think I am," I said.

The woman shook her head. She retreated into the shadowy hallway of the house and placed the tulips somewhere out of sight. Then, without another word, she shut the door.

I walked quickly back through the picket fence and almost crossed the street. Almost.

Something made me look at the basement doors. One was open just a crack. In all the times my mother and I had passed the house, neither had ever been open. I stepped off the sidewalk and into the street, edging along the curb, wanting and not wanting to see what I might see.

Something glowed in there. Something yellowish and greenish, and it was moving, shifting, curling around the door like snake, so faint that it was nearly translucent, but I saw it. I wanted to run toward and from it in the same moment.

The door opened wider. There was the woman again.

"Come," she said, reaching out her hand. "Come see. Come, mon amie."

I ran. I ran all the way home and flung open the door of my house. I ran straight into my mother.

"Where have you been?" she asked in her you've-been-up-to-something-haven't-you voice. She was angry. I could've been hurt somewhere or kidnapped. Or eaten.

I couldn't stop shivering. My mother fussed over me, looking for cuts, bruises, scrapes needing antibiotic ointment. I wished what had happened, what I'd seen, could be rubbed away, rubbed from my eyes, from my memory. Was the old woman crazy or was I? What had she wanted to show me? What kind of coward was I that I ran from her? Did I really believe there was something in that basement?

"I'd tell you," I said, "but you should be careful what you let in your head. You can't get it back out.

"Not ever."

My mother eyed me carefully.

"And sometimes, Mom, that's a good thing."

WELCOME TO CHARIHO: RHODE ISLAND'S ROSWELL

When the alien invasion happens, it will occur in Wood River Junction. Perhaps at night. In the vicinity of Route 1 near the United Nuclear Corporation plant. And the little green men will likely arrive in pancake-shaped crafts that make ocean dives.

Seriously. I have it on good authority.

That is, if the invasion hasn't happened already. We may have missed it. In fact, aliens may well be among us, working at your kids' schools, playing basketball with your husband at the Y, taking your daughter to the prom. Find your neighbor a little odd? You might not know the half of it. You could be chatting up ET for all you know.

Especially if you're living in South County. The Rhode Island UFO Reports Page—yes, seriously, it exists—has South County ranking first in Rhode Island for number of reported UFO sightings: forty-five. Providence is second with twenty-two, and Newport County is third with thirteen. History indicates it's highly unlikely that you'll see a UFO in Kent or Bristol Counties. Their sightings records are meager: Kent, five, and Bristol, three. Recordkeeping dates back to August 1964, when Charlestown residents reported seeing a bright light, like a star, rise up out of the ocean at a forty-five-degree angle, zigzag a bit and then shoot straight up into the sky.

But the big UFO year was '73. In February 1973, no fewer than 250 residents of Wood River Junction witnessed a bit of weirdness in the night sky. The following is from the May 1973 issue of *UFO Investigator*:

Feb., 1973, Wood River Junction, RI
*Day after day, week after week numerous residents claim that they have
seen a "huge bright white light," moving slowly above their community.
More than 250 people have reportedly seen the object since it was first
sighted in February. The UFO has been observed by many residents
hovering soundlessly at tree-top [sic] level for minutes at a time before
disappearing. Many have claimed the object is huge, with estimates
ranging from "bigger than a car" to ½ the size of a house. A number
of the sightings according to local reports have occurred near the United
Nuclear Corp. plant located nearby. United Nuclear operates a waste
reclamation plant. Witnesses to these sightings have reported observing
what appear to be military aircraft searching or patrolling the area
following UFO sightings. Thomas Gariepy, a reporter for the Providence
Evening Bulletin, is among those residents who have observed a UFO
in recent months.*

Most assuredly, *UFO Investigator* carries the clout of the *New York Times*
for its target demographic. Curious, though, as to why this *Close Encounters
of the Third Kind*–esque event was not covered by mainstream media. Two
hundred and fifty people see a house-sized light hovering above treetops
and no media coverage? Must have been a big news month for that to
have failed to attract attention.

Then came the following a month later in the May/June 1973 edition
of the *APRO Bulletin*:

April 10, 1973, City not noted, RI
*A woman driving along U.S. highway 1 in southern Rhode Island saw
a reddish-orange object move toward her car, then pass directly overhead.
Her car lights dimmed and the engine faltered. The object was estimated
to be 42 feet in diameter, and was surrounded by a green haze.*

So 251 people see strange things in the night sky in South County in
the winter and spring of 1973. Disturbing? Yes. Unusual? Depends on
whom you talk to.

UFOs, The X-Files *and the Allure of Lobsters*

In May 1996, the season finale of the Fox television show *The X-Files* ended with the show's lead characters, two FBI agents named Fox Mulder and Dana Scully, witnessing two aliens face off in a spaghetti-western-style showdown under an overpass on Interstate 95 in Rhode Island. *The X-Files*, a wildly popular Golden Globe Award–winning show in the 1990s, chronicled agents Mulder and Scully's investigations of crimes with supernatural aspects. Many episodes centered on the pair's investigation of alien visitations, as Mulder was forever trying to learn what had happened to his sister, who had been abducted by aliens when he was a teenager. The show was filmed in Vancouver, Canada, and set in Washington, D.C. So, when their investigation leads Fox and Scully to Quonochontaug, Rhode Island, there's the question of why.

Quonochontaug is a tony beach community in Charlestown, neighbor to Richmond and, according to *The X-Files*, one of the places aliens have scouted out in their plans for mass colonization of Earth. Some, Fox and Scully learn, have been summering there for more than two decades, alongside the Mulders, who have a beach cottage there. In the season finale, Mulder's mom has a stroke and is taken to a Providence hospital by Westerly's Shelter Harbor Rescue.

At the time of the show's airing, I placed a call to the producers of *The X-Files*. The publicist said she did not know if there was any significance to the choice of Quonochontaug as the setting for the alien faceoff. "Normally, the places chosen for the shows are at random," she said.

At random? Really? Don't think so. Quonochontaug is smack dab in the middle of alien country.

In 1996, the Ocean State Job Lot Plaza on Route 138 in Richmond was the Rhode Island headquarters for the UFO Lab Museum. And it was there for a reason. Richmond, home to Rhode Island's largest fair, the Washington County Fair, and the largest school district, Wood River Junction's Chariho Regional School District, is, as has already been established, a hotbed of alleged alien activity.

So, at random, really? Conspiracy theorists would beg to differ.

Monsters' Lairs

"A Big Flap Year"

In 1996, I asked Don Todd, a retired military man and Wakefield-based UFO investigator affiliated with the Mutual UFO Network (MUFON), about Quonochontaug and its alien visitation history, if any. He could recall only one report. It was in 1973, "a big flap year," he said. "Flap" is shorthand for "flapjack," used to describe a saucer-shaped UFO. UFOs can also be shaped like cigars. Todd, who spent half a century investigating these sightings before retiring in 1994, evaluated more than two hundred cases. Quonochontaug is fiercely and deliberately secluded, with more private property notices than street signs, which could explain why it's a preferred destination for alien visitation. Quonochontaug people respect one another's privacy.

The Quonny case involved a UFO that "came in from out over the ocean, hovered, dropped down like an elevator going floor to floor and then tilted and dove into the water," Todd said. "It was an obvious dive. It's a good maneuver of theirs; the water's a good place to hide."

So true.

I went looking for Quonochontaug residents who might be willing to talk about the prospect of alien invasion. The Munger sisters, Terry and Bobbie, of West End Road, retirees and summer residents of Quonny for more than thirty-five years, thought their community a dubious destination for alien occupation.

"There's no place to land a UFO here," Terry said. "They couldn't colonize in the marshes. The state would kick them out."

"Maybe they could just hover?" Bobbie suggested.

"They probably come for the lobster, for the fishing," Bobbie added. "They wouldn't come just for the scenery. That's boring."

I refrain from telling them that human beings are the preferred food source in most alien invasion scenarios. Lobsters likely run a distant second.

"I'd probably recognize them if they were here," Terry mused.

"Well, I don't know. I think they'd look very normal," Bobbie said.

"Don't they have big, round, bald heads and great big eyes?" Terry asked.

"No, they'd look like us," Bobbie replied. "I think they'd be normal and come in fishing clothes."

"How big a colony is this, anyway?" Terry asked.

Bobbie wondered aloud if Quonochontaug's recent construction boom and a number of houses' use of Doric columns on their façades offered any clues to the alien mystery. Given aliens' use of columns of light to transport to and from the mother ship, Doric columns took on ominous implications. Perhaps they were here.

"That's all we need," said Terry. "Aliens in Quonochontaug."

Update: Don Todd's whereabouts in 2011, the time of the writing of this book, are unknown. *The X-Files* became one of the longest-running science fiction television shows in history before signing off in 2002. Actress Gillian Anderson went on to star in the PBS production of Charles Dickens's *Bleak House*. *The X-Files* male lead David Duchovny does voiceovers for Pedigree dog food, stars in the Showtime series *Californication* and has been in and out of rehab for sex addiction. The UFO Lab Museum is closed, and the Rhode Island chapter of MUFON is now part of New England MUFON. And the UFO Lab Museum's URL, www.ufolabri.com, takes you to a Chinese e-commerce site selling jams, jellies and marmalades.

THE TALE OF THE CRYING BOG

The fog lay a foot above the bog, a heavy blanket, silver in the moonlight, somnolently undulating and swirling, making it impossible for the girl to see her steps. Several times she stumbled over the uneven terrain, struggling against the mud and muck, trying to swallow her sobbing, humming tunelessly to the two newborns she held in her arms.

She was grateful for the pain in her flanks; it kept her from falling asleep even though she was exhausted. She would have to sit down; the babies were wailing, their little bodies rigid with fury. Cold, hungry and sticky with afterbirth, they demanded to be fed. Their noise might attract fisher cats or wolves, and the girl was too weak to fight anything they might meet in the bog.

A child herself, she hardly knew what to do with the infants, her children, a boy and a girl. She sat heavily, the ground squelching beneath her, and bared her chest right there in the fog and the dark, pressing one and then the other child to her aching breasts. The pain of their latching made her jump and cry out, but then came relief. She cried silently for this small favor, one less bit of misery. Maybe the gods had taken pity on her. Soon, she had a sleeping baby on each arm. Then she, too, slept.

Awake. Her head snapped up, and she was alert. To what? The marsh's quiet was broken only by the croaks, screeches and splashes of unseen night creatures. But she was frightened. The babies awoke and latched on to her again. Now she started at every snap of a twig, every footfall on leaves. A squirrel or a bird could make a noise loud enough to sound like a much larger animal; she knew this, but still she tensed, curling her back, folding the babies into her, wishing the fog would hide her like it did all the other inhabitants of the bog. How long had she slept? She would have to wait until morning to get out. She was still too tired, and it was too dark to risk walking. One misstep and she could put all three of them under water.

She looked at the faces of the babies and wondered if they looked like her. Or him. Where was he? He said he'd be back. Her Frenchman. She remembered her father's face, ugly with anger, spitting the name of her beloved from his mouth, as if the words held the taste of something rancid. Her mother, bitter with the knowledge that her daughter had shamed the family—and would not be adding to it with a husband who could care for her elderly parents—could not bear to look at her. In the last months of her waiting, when her stomach had swelled obscenely, her parents turned her out of their home. And when her tribe learned of her shameful secret, she was shunned, an outcast, driven out to wander, to beg and then, finally, to steal to eat.

When she felt the first pains of birth, she went to the bog, wading through the cold, dank water to the island where she and the young

French officer had had all of their meetings. Where he had promised he would return. But he didn't, so she delivered her babies alone, screaming in pain and terror, no one to help her understand what was happening.

She'd wrapped her children in her deerskin and shakily risen. The stink of the blood and gore was certain to attract animals. She had to move, to find some sort of shelter. Had she gone far enough? She could not tell. Now she sat, despairing, bloodied and broken, cold and wet, stinking of sweat and urine, tears blending with the dank, wet air that hung heavy around her. She'd walked a few steps at most. She needed rest, time to gather her strength. Hugging her sleeping babies to her, she closed her eyes. She must sleep again.

The whistle woke her.

She jolted, and the babies stirred. She placed one to each breast and drew up her knees protectively against their backs, a clumsy, vulnerable position, but she had to keep them quiet. She had to be sure she'd heard it. It was still dark, but to the east there was the thinnest ribbon of rosy light. The babies latched on and suckled, and she waited for the sound. Had it been a dream?

Then. Again. A whistle—almost the same as the one her lover had made to announce his arrival. But that was a clear, sweet sound, and this was not. There was something eerie in the notes, something frightening.

She hunched over her babies, and her mind raced. To move was to risk their crying out; to stay was to risk the thing getting closer. *Don't think, don't think, don't think.* But the stories would come. Of Hobomok, the vengeful god with an appetite for human flesh, and his brother, It, who dwelt and hunted in the swamps, marshes and bogs. And the ghosts. And the wolves, the snakes and other things unimaginable.

The whistle again. Closer, but from where? Behind her? In front of her? The fog made it impossible to see, and now her ears failed her. She felt a tug and then cool air on her breast. The infant girl—*she must name them*—had fallen off, asleep again. The boy child still worked her breast.

"Tu es à moi." You are mine.

Her breath caught in her throat.

The whisper again.

"You are mine."

The girl's mind raced—could it be him? But no. It wasn't right. What he was saying wasn't quite right. Her French soldier always said, "Tu es à moi, l'amour (You are mine, love)." Again, the voice.

"You are mine. You are mine. You are mine. You are mine!"

The voice grew less human with each repetition. The words lost their meaning, so filled were they with menace.

"Mine. Mine. Mine. Mine."

She struggled to her feet. Her body was so sore, but she ran. She ran from the voice, both her babies crying out in anger at the jostling. *Run! Hide!* She ran toward the sunrise, toward the abandoned beaver dam, a ruin of mud and sticks, a favorite place for snakes to sun themselves in the summer. There was a hole in the dam, a hollowed-out place. The girl wedged herself into the twigs and mud and prayed the demon would miss her.

Then the baby boy bellowed. She hugged him to her chest, pressing his tiny face to her bosom, willing him to be quiet. The girl stayed sleeping. Up again. Crashing through the den. The babies bellowing. She stumbled, nearly fell and just avoided plunging into the water. The voice was behind her, gaining on her.

"Mine. Mine. Mine. Mine."

She held her breath as she heard the thing crashing through the bog. It approached the den; she could feel it. And its smell was pungent, a stink of sulfur.

"Mine." A whisper, a cackle. Behind her? She whirled around. Nothing. "Mine." *Was it her imagination, or was the voice fainter?* "Mine." A whisper.

She laughed. She looked to the east; the sun had cleared the horizon. The night thing had no power in the presence of light. She smiled and praised her gods, the Christian gods, all of them. Then she looked down. Her first glimpse of her babies' faces by daylight.

It took her a moment to understand. At first, it looked like they were just sleeping. *Not dead! No, not dead!* She put her ear to the girl's mouth and then to the boy's. Lips so blue. *They were sleeping. They had to be.* But no.

"Mine."

She screamed until she had no voice. Then she waded into the tall grass and headed to where the swans bedded down, laid their eggs. Beautiful creatures should be with other beautiful creatures. With slow, deliberate movements, she placed the girl and then the boy into the water. They were pure, and the water took them as it did all holy things. So the Christians said, and they were right. Hobomok could not take them now. She would lay down with them, die now if she could, but she was unworthy. She had killed her children.

Great sacrifice was required to restore honor.

She headed for the ocean.

When she reached the beach, the Indian maiden climbed out onto the jetty. She stripped off her clothing and knelt, praying to her gods once more, imploring their forgiveness. An immense rock rose from the ocean, and the Indian maiden looked at it in wonder and gladness. The gods had granted her a means of absolution. The Indian maiden smiled. She stood, turned and ran the length of the jetty, placing as much distance between herself and the rock as she could. Then, she ran toward it. When she neared the jetty's end, she raised her hands above her and joined them, palm to palm, fingers pressed tightly together, as she'd seen the Puritans do. Without a word, she took aim for the rock and dove. She hit the rock headfirst, her skull smashing, her neck breaking on impact.

She awoke in the bog. It was nightfall again, and her arms ached. But there were no babies in her arms. Had the gods not been pleased with her sacrifice? Had she not restored her honor and that of her family? She had given her life. It was all she had. The sadness and rage rose within her until she erupted, a volcanic bellowing, a ghastly screaming that set birds to flight. She raged on, taunting, baiting the thing that had chased her, that had taken her babies' lives, inviting it to take her, too. But where? What could be worse than this hell of her own making?

When she could screech no more, she fell to her knees and stayed there. No crying, no praying. Then, ever so faintly, came a noise. Not the sound of a monster but the shrill cry of a hungry baby. Was it north? East? She was not sure. She stilled herself. Again, the cry. But this time, it came from behind her. The south. Definitely. But no. A third cry. North. The cries were coming from the north.

Once again, she scanned the horizon, trying to take in the near, the far, all the sounds and movements. How much commotion could two babies make? Somehow they'd become separated. No matter. She was alive. So they were alive, too. Somewhere close. She would find them both. She walked deeper into the bog, wading into the serpentine mist that rose to greet her until, finally, it swallowed her whole.

And when the moon cycles into fullness and a low-lying fog creeps along the ground, some say they can hear the Indian maiden sobbing still, looking for her lost infants in the Crying Bog.

Others hear something different. A single word: "Mine."

HOW THE DEVIL CAME TO DO GOD'S WORK

In the early days, when Quebecois farmhouses were common sites in Woonsocket and religious devotion ran deep, there was a small, devout congregation of French Canadians who wanted to build a church for their *curé*, their priest. They were poor folk, though, and lacked the horsepower for the church of their dreams: an impressive stone church to rival those in the cities.

But one dark night, their priest was awakened. Before him was a woman of unearthly beauty and majesty, the Blessed Virgin herself. He fell to his knees at the sight of her.

"My Son has heard your prayers, and He would have you build your stone church. But you do not have animals strong enough to haul the stone you will need. And so I will send you a horse. He is no ordinary animal. He will do the work of twenty great horses in a single day. He will require no water and no food. Put him to work for as long as you need him."

The priest nodded and thanked the Virgin.

"There is just one thing you must remember: the horse will wear a special bridle, and you are forbidden to remove it."

The priest nodded.

"If you or someone else takes the bridle from his head, the horse will bolt, and you will be left without a way to finish your church. And tell no one of my visit or of the special nature of this horse," the Blessed Mother said. "He is not of this world."

The Virgin then began to ascend, sheathed in a blinding light. The priest shielded his eyes for just a moment, but when he lifted his hand from his brow, the Holy Mother was gone. The priest stayed on his knees for most of the night, praying and thanking the Virgin, before finally succumbing to sleep at dawn. He dreamed of a great white steed and a church so magnificent it seemed made of precious metal and jewels.

An angry neighing awoke him several hours later. The tired priest went to the door of his small home, and outside, tethered to his little iron gate, was the largest, blackest, fiercest horse he had ever seen. Scarier even than his massiveness, though, were the horse's eyes. They were angry. The beast seemed to glare at the priest, and the holy man was afraid. If the animal were to rear up, the priest knew he'd lift that little iron gate off its hinges with no more effort than it took the wind to move a fallen leaf. But for all its distemper, the horse submitted to its lot and allowed the priest to take the reins and walk it to the worksite, where the parishioners labored.

The priest gave the horse to the foreman, a pious, trustworthy man who did not question him when the holy man said it was a gift from God. That the horse was here today but not yesterday was no business of his. The foreman trusted his priest, even when the holy man forbade him to remove the horse's bridle. The foreman noted that the horse's bit was far too tight; wrinkles bunched on either side of the beast's mouth. The animal had to be in pain. And the bit was so large that it would make drinking difficult for the animal. The foreman was a softhearted man who took good care of his own animals.

"Father, I have a question," the man said.

The priest nodded.

"You say, don't remove the bridle, but what about loosening it? It's too tight, and I fear the animal is in pain."

The priest frowned. He couldn't explain. He had promised the Virgin.

"I forbid you to remove the bridle," he told the foreman. "He is a very strong beast, and we will lose control of him. And I promise you, we'll not have him back."

The foreman nodded. He would not challenge the priest's answer.

"Then all I ask, Father, is if I might know his name?"

The priest paused. The Virgin had not named the horse.

"Old Nick. If you must call him something, call him Old Nick."

The foreman crossed himself. "Mon Dieu, Father. You have brought us the devil to build our church?"

The priest sighed and shook his head. He hadn't intended to say "Old Nick." He'd been compelled to. Confused, he looked at the horse. It snorted. An answer? He wondered.

"It is what it is," he said to the foreman, handing him the reins. "Use a different name if you wish."

Like the priest, the foreman marveled that a horse that seemed to seethe with anger should be so easily led. He hauled more stone than a dozen horses could in a day and never resisted work, even when the foreman feared he'd pushed the horse past the bearable. All was progressing ahead of schedule, and the church that they had feared would not be done by winter seemed certain to be built by early fall.

If only Batisse Champlain had not interfered.

Now, it was the understanding among the crew that only the foreman would handle the horse. But one day, he was sick. And that day extended into a week. His wife said she could not understand what was wrong with him. "He talks of a red-eyed, fire-breathing horse coming to drag him to hell," she told the priest. "My husband is a good man. He has not done anything that would weigh so on his soul, that would invite a demon's visit."

When the foreman was gone a month, the priest, who tethered the horse to his gate every night since its arrival, visited the building site. Only a few days' work remained for the horse. The priest asked for a volunteer to handle the horse in the foreman's absence.

Most of the men were reluctant. They believed Old Nick was the horse that tormented the foreman as he slept. They feared that if they were to take the reins, his fate would be theirs as well. Only Batisse Chamberlain thought otherwise.

"Father, I will take charge of the horse until our foreman is back."

The priest was wary. Batisse was a braggart, a boaster, someone who thought he knew better than others. But there were no other volunteers.

"I entrust you with this horse, Batisse, but you must do as I say. You cannot remove his bridle, ever. You may think me cruel, but you must not disobey. Do not take his bridle off."

Batisse agreed to the priest's command and abided by it. For a day.

It was a hot summer. That day, the men sweated so profusely that their clothes were soaked, and they stripped their shirts for relief. By dusk, Batisse had a brutal sunburn and a throat so parched he could not give direction to man or horse. Batisse led the horse to a nearby river. He stripped and entered the water, gulping it until his stomach was distended.

The horse stood in the mud next to the river. Untethered, it stared at Batisse. With its eyes half closed and strands of spittle hanging like icicles from its mouth, the horse looked like a rabid animal. Batisse felt not pity but fear of the horse for the first time. It seemed silly, but he felt that Old Nick wished to harm him. He had to make peace with the beast. He shivered despite the heat and left the water. Grabbing the horse's reins, he led Old Nick into the river.

"Drink now," he urged the horse. But it did not—even when Batisse tried to shove the horse's mouth into the water. Nor would he take water from Batisse's cupped hand.

"It's that damn bridle," Batisse said. He sighed. "What harm can there be in taking it off this one time? You are far too exhausted to run. To hell with the priest."

Batisse withdrew the bridle and its bit from the horse's mouth.

"No!" screamed a voice from behind him. Batisse turned to see the foreman in his nightshirt running toward him, arms outstretched, eyes wide with horror.

Batisse turned to the horse, fearful that the foreman's behavior would spook it. For his reward, he received a hoof to the chest so forceful that he shot into the air and landed with a hard *thwack* on the muddy riverbank. As he struggled to get up, Batisse watched as the horse reared up and leapt across the wide river, landing on a ledge overhanging it. The ledge and land that supported it cracked beneath the beast's hooves, and Old Nick dropped down into the deep cleft rent open.

Batisse ran after the horse until he was out of breath and doubled over in pain. But it was no use. No man, nor horse, would overtake the beast. He made his way to the priest's home to share his shameful news. But the priest, who had been out visiting a sick parishioner, had met the demon horse on the road, and when Batisse arrived at the priest's gate, he found the holy man on his knees praying. The priest rocked back and forth, moaning and asking the Virgin Mary for forgiveness. Batisse did not understand the full meaning of the priest's prayers but heard enough to know he'd let loose something far more dangerous than an untamed horse.

"Mon Dieu, Father, what have I done?" Batisse asked.

The priest shook his head. "You could not know, Batisse. It is my burden."

Further explanation was prevented by the arrival of the foreman. He looked more wraith than man, with his wide eyes and unkempt hair. When he saw Batisse, the foreman stopped and pointed, staring at him with such hatred that the other man cowered. "You have let him loose on us," the foreman shouted at Batisse. "You have set the devil free!"

The priest tried to calm the foreman, but he would not be pacified.

"Father, I saw him leap the width of the river and cleave the land in two. He has opened the gates of hell, Father. He will have all our souls!" the foreman cried.

The priest told Batisse to go home and took the foreman back to his wife. Then he climbed Fairmount Hill and found the chasm where Old Nick was said to have made his way home. The holy man found no further sign of the beast. Then, in his solitude, he, too, cried and gnashed his teeth and suffered as his foreman had suffered. Had Old Nick found a way to come and go from hell itself? Would he return for them? The priest despaired. He had been given a great gift by the Virgin herself, and he had not only failed but also imperiled all who would be guided by him. The priest was never the same again.

Nor was Fairmount Hill and its chasm.

Though the people of village did not see signs of a demon horse, they felt his presence when in the vicinity of the chasm they called Devil's Hole. No living thing would tarry there. Horses made to travel there would be lamed. Wagons would lose their wheels. And the man foolish enough to travel there at nighttime would return with tales of unholy moans, terrible shrieks and glowing, red eyes. Some even said they'd been chased by a black wolf that breathed fire.

Eventually, a new priest arrived, and when he heard tales of Devil's Hole, he recruited a group of the bravest villagers to visit the unholy sight. Because he was a holy man and loved by his parishioners, they laid aside their guns and took up hammers and nails instead. At the site where Old Nick had struck the rock and descended into hell, the priest had his congregants build and erect a cross. Then, together, they prayed, and the priest blessed the ground. It was said that all in the little party repented their sins and pledged never to take another drink. And it would seem that their offerings were accepted, for no evil has happened since at Devil's Hole.

THE DEVIL AND OLD RICHARD COREY

The day before the night Old Richard Corey met the devil was an ordinary one.

Old Richard Corey set out at twilight from Hazard Farm after at least a half day's honest work. He never took the quickest route home, opting instead to enter Wilson's Woods, a half mile northeast of Benny Rodman's Mill. Richard was scared to take a more direct route, for one evening he'd run into a rather large and unique snake near the mill. Old Man Corey had been gathering huckleberries when he came upon it—a snake black as coal and as long as a fence rail. "Twenty feet, on my honor," Richard Corey would say to anyone who'd listen.

But that was not the strangest thing about the snake, he'd add, shaking his hoary head. This snake had a jewel in the center of its head, a third eye; a yellow diamond as big as a teakettle. His friends found this terribly funny. Old Richard Corey was a teller of tall tales and a lazy bastard, always skulking around Hazard Farm with his shovel in hand because he'd heard rumors Captain William Kidd had buried treasure on the property. Surely, if he'd come across a snake with a jeweled head, he would have brained that snake with that shovel or died trying. But Richard Corey just shook his head. He had a respect for God's and the devil's creatures, and that snake surely belonged to Old Nick.

And so it was that Old Richard Corey, shovel in hand, entered Wilson's Woods like he did every other day, except Sundays. At first, nothing seemed amiss. There were the usual long shadows and the cries of night creatures waking. Richard always picked up the pace a little bit when things started stirring. Even the sound of his own feet shuffling through brittle oak leaves

Artist's rendering of pirate William Kidd. *Illustration by Howard Pyle.*

made him flinch. A snapped branch could make him jump straight up into the air. And so Richard Corey whistled, a loud, shrill sound like a gull's call, to drown out the night's screeches and croaks. He also dosed himself with more than a few draughts of whiskey from a flask he kept on hand. For medicinal purposes, he'd say to those who witnessed him.

In the middle of Wilson's Woods was a small clearing—a glade with grass that was never browned by sun or blemished by toadstools or even fallen leaves. It was like a carpet. And it was here, in what would be known forevermore as the Devil's Ring, that Richard Corey met the Master of Lies.

He did not know, at first, that the thing was the devil. He thought maybe it was Benny Nichols's big black bull that charged him. Until the thing stood upright and grabbed him around the waist.

Richard Corey, who dropped his shovel the instant he saw the creature, hollered and flailed his arms. His feet found no ground to move him. He went limp, playing dead, and then stiff when the creature spoke: "I hear you are the biggest liar who ever lived, which is a problem for me," the devil hissed. "I don't like to be outdone."

The devil's large nostrils flared, twin furnaces, threatening to melt the massive gold ring piercing them. Even in his terror, Old Richard Corey wondered what such a ring would be worth.

"I am the Father of Lies. I am the Prince of Prevarication," the devil thundered. "But you, you mewling, puny, poor excuse for a man. You have people saying you would best even me."

Richard Corey cowered.

"So I've come to take you to hell," the devil said, his voice going smooth and almost gentlemanly. "You'll be in good company down there, and all will be right again up here."

He tucked Richard Corey under his arm as if he carried a piglet. And, in piglet fashion, Richard Corey squealed himself hoarse.

He begged and pleaded with the devil. He'd change. He'd stop lying. He'd be a more selective sinner. Take on new vices. Lie less but drink and gamble more, just to keep all in balance. You have to be careful negotiating penance with the devil, Richard Corey thought. Can't promise to become a good person; after all, that'd just make him angrier.

The devil snorted as he carried Richard Corey away from Wilson's Woods, across Tug Bog and Sot's Hole, toward the Great Swamp, which, everyone knew, was a favorite destination of all manner of godless creatures. The old man despaired. Nothing good ever came of a walk through the Great Swamp at night.

The devil slowed his pace as he entered the swamp.

Old Richard Corey begged some more.

"Please, I can change. I can tell a few truths."

"You're a liar. I'd be a fool to believe you."

"Yes, I'm a liar, your…" Richard Corey struggled to find the right words to address the devil. To call the creature "Prince" or "Majesty" could buy him some time but might, if he were facing imminent death, put him on the wrong side of the Almighty. And he wasn't sure God was going to feel much differently toward him than the devil. Flattery wasn't his strong suit anyway. People just thought he was lying to get his way with something, and they were right.

The old man tried a different tactic.

"I'm a liar, but I'm not the worst liar alive."

"So you're saying there's one worse than you?"

"Yes, sir, I am."

The devil considered this as he dangled Richard Corey at the edge of Genesee Brook. He lowered the old man just enough that Richard Corey's feet touched the ground. Then what was beneath him moved, and the old man tried to scrabble up the devil like a scared baby would its mother.

The devil snorted his disgust.

Richard Corey's mind reeled. Why the devil would take issue with a liar made no sense. Maybe he didn't, really. Maybe he was playing with the old man. Then again, the devil was the embodiment of evil. Why wouldn't he be a jealous and competitive cur? It would explain what happened next. The devil turned Old Richard Corey around so that the two were eye to eye, nose to flaring nostrils.

"Is that so? You know a liar worse than you?" The devil growled, growing, it seemed, more monstrous and malevolent with each passing moment. Old Man Corey could not miss the contempt in his words. The devil was a coil, a breath away from springing. To hell? Richard Corey fought the urge to cross himself. Bad form.

The devil asked, "Would you lie to me even now?"

Richard Corey just whimpered. They were nose to nostrils again. He was pretty sure his eyebrows had been singed.

The devil tucked Richard Corey back under his arm and, in one leap, returned to the Devil's Ring, where he set the shaken man down.

"Well, if that's true, then my grievance is not with you, Richard Corey. But you will need to prove yourself truthful this time. I want you to bring the man or woman whom you say is a bigger liar. Tomorrow night. Here. To the Devil's Ring. Who is this liar?"

Richard Corey stammered. "Old Paris Garner of Tefft Hill is a bigger liar."

The devil snorted, laughed and ripped a six-foot-long trench underneath his left hoof. Clearly, the devil found this funny. "You bring this Paris Garner back here, Richard Corey. Don't come back here without him."

And then Richard Corey found himself alone once more in Devil's Ring.

The next day, Richard Corey made a big production of digging holes in the turf on the outskirts of Thomas Hazard's farm. Paris Garner, who on his best day could barely abide by the laziness and greed of Richard Corey, marched over and pulled the shovel from his hands.

"Richard Corey, if you don't do something useful, I'll see that Thomas Hazard puts you off his land forever."

Richard Corey wiped his brow. Digging holes all day had been tough work, but here in front of him was the prize.

"Paris, I hadn't wanted to share, but I need your help, and I promise, if you do, we'll both be richer than Thomas Hazard," he said.

Paris Garner snorted.

"How's that, Corey?"

"I found something, Paris," Corey whispered. "Treasure, I think, but I need the help of a trusted friend."

Paris made a show of looking over his shoulder. "Don't see any friends here, Corey," he said.

The old man scowled. "Well, you'll have to do because I need to get this out of the ground before someone else does. I think I found the treasure Captain Kidd buried here."

"That's just an old wives' tale," Paris scoffed. "Old Lady Watson been telling you about the voices she hears up at Sugarloaf Hill? Kidd's buried treasure up there, too, or so she says. Better bring yer shovel, though. I hear there's a big, black snake up there, too. Story goes that every time the snake appears, the treasure sinks lower into the earth. So you'll have to kill it quick."

Paris laughed. He knew how the old man felt about snakes. Richard Corey scowled.

"Fine. I'll get someone else. I was gonna split it with you. There's enough to make the two of us very rich men."

Now, Paris had heard rumors that the Thomas B. Hazard house was a haven for pirates who plagued the American and West Indian seas, and the Hazard family, it was said, had plowed up strange and foreign treasure from time to time. The most interesting loot was the brass handle of a broadsword bearing the name Artemus Gould, pirate.

Could Corey be telling the truth? Paris shook his head but said nothing.

Old Richard Corey took the other man's silence as encouragement and continued.

"I think it's a keg of gold," he said.

He grabbed Paris with filthy hands. The other man looked at Richard Corey's grubby claws. Underneath his nails were half moons of inky dirt. It looked fairly fresh. Had the man really found something?

"I think the dread pirate William Kidd buried a keg of gold in Devil's Ring," Corey said. "I've seen the keg, but there are bones on top of it. Kidd's said to have killed a man and laid his body on top of every treasure he sunk in the ground," Corey said. "I need help moving the bones."

Paris Garner shook his head and laughed.

"I don't know what you're up to, old man, but I ain't going anywhere near Devil's Ring with you, and I certainly ain't disturbing the dead. You can keep your treasure."

Paris Garner retrieved Old Richard Corey's shovel.

"Take your shovel and take you treasure," he said and smiled. "You're welcome to my share."

Old Richard Corey never returned to the Devil's Ring or Wilson's Woods, for that matter. And while the devil did eventually come for him, it was long after the appointed date. Some said that Paris Garner was the devil in the woods that night and that he'd had a bit of fun with Old Richard Corey. Others, those who believed the devil walked freely among them, avoided Wilson's Woods and the Devil's Ring, believing it best to avoid fire-breathing devils and big black snakes—even if they did wear gold and diamonds.

THE UNFORTUNATE HANNAH ROBINSON

They called her unfortunate in that way people do when they don't mean what they say. When they're secretly delighted with another's misfortune but fearful they'll be found out. So they honeyed their words with false sympathy, rubbed their dry eyes red and put hands to their mouths to hide the satisfied smiles. The best of the worst of them even managed a tear or two.

Hannah would not have been surprised, for the whispers about Hannah Robinson started long before she died.

At first, it was just embarrassing gossip: tales of an American heiress so beautiful that she outshone the queen of England. Later, though, came the humiliating stories. In these, she was a cliché, the "unfortunate" Hannah Robinson, just another naïve girl ruined by a scoundrel. Then, in death, she was a wraith, a specter, a ghost story.

In life and death, Hannah Robinson was a legend.

She had the good fortune of being not only singularly beautiful but also very, very rich. She was a prize to be won. And the bidding was fierce.

Men were silly around her—waxing on about Hannah's Grecian features, writing poetry about her pale skin, auburn hair and dark, hazel eyes. But Hannah took no pride in her appearance. She was a virtuous girl betrayed by looks that gave men unwholesome thoughts. As a child, Hannah had put molasses in her hair to try to blacken her auburn curls. She heard that the biblical whore Mary Magdalene had red hair and feared people would think the resemblance ran deeper than the physical.

So when Hannah's friends talked about this or that soldier who confessed to loving them, she kept quiet. Her friends couldn't understand it. The stories she could tell! Everyone knew, not from Hannah's telling but because her sister Mary had witnessed it, that crazy Colonel Harry Babcock, who kissed the queen of England full on the mouth, had said when meeting Hannah, "Permit, dear Madame, the lips that have kissed unrebuked those of the proudest queen of earth, to press, for a moment, the hand of an angel of heaven." Hannah thought the whole episode ridiculous and mortifying. If one of her friends even so much as said "Crazy Harry," Hannah would be up and out of the room in a moment.

Some wondered if this wasn't Hannah's way of drawing attention to herself. Wasn't it enough to be beautiful and wealthy? Must she always make a spectacle of herself? Those who hated Hannah—and there were a few—delighted in her downfall, saying hers were the actions of a hussy. Not that they were surprised, mind you; she had to have done something to drive men so crazy. They wondered aloud how her poor parents were dealing with the shame she'd brought the family. "Unfortunate Hannah," they'd hiss when out of earshot. It was her parents who were the unfortunate ones. The only good turn she'd done them was dying young.

Hannah Robinson fell in love with Pierre "Peter" Simons for the same reasons that all girls did: He was young. He was handsome. And he was tragic. The son of upper-class Huguenots, Peter and his family had fled their homeland because of religious persecution. In the colonies, Peter was a dance master at Madame Osborne's finishing school in Newport. Hannah, who'd been staying in the city with her uncle's family, was his student.

All involved in the sordidness that followed did agree on one point: an heiress's marriage to a foreigner, and a Frenchman and a dancing master was not what Rowland Robinson wanted for his beloved daughter. But Hannah's uncle, William Gardiner, and his children liked Peter very much, so much that Uncle William retained him as a tutor. This allowed Peter and Hannah's relationship to grow. Then Hannah's mother, Anstis, became so taken with him that she convinced her husband to have Peter tutor Hannah and her sister. By the time Mrs. Robinson realized that Hannah's teacher was her lover, she was a bit in love with the boy herself. She even allowed Peter into the girls' bedroom, while she chaperoned, of course. Mr. Robinson had no idea of the romance. The girls' bedroom contained a small closet next to the hearth in which Peter would hide if he happened to be up there when Mr. Robinson entered the house.

Above: Hannah Robinson's bedroom, Narragansett. *Photo by author*.

Left: The closet where Hannah Robinson's lover hid, Narragansett. *Photo by author*.

Hannah and Peter were discovered when Mr. Robinson found the tutor hidden in a lilac bush below Hannah's window. Hannah had dropped a note for Peter into the lilac bush, as was their habit. Mr. Robinson used his walking cane to flush his prey from the bush. The enraged father forbid Hannah to leave her home without a servant's supervision. Mom Anstis clearly could not be trusted.

And the story might have ended there but for a ball Lodowick Updike threw at Smith's Castle in Wickford. Because Updike was a relative, Mr. Robinson allowed Hannah and her sister to attend, accompanied by his trusted servant, Prince. The two daughters left on horseback with Prince. One returned. Peter knew of the plan, intercepted the party and took Hannah to Providence, where they were married.

But the happily ever after was short-lived. Hannah was disowned and Peter disinterested when he discovered he'd married a penniless woman. He took to drinking, gambling and womanizing. He abandoned Hannah. Two years after the elopement, Rowland and Anstis learned that Hannah was gravely ill. They feared the worst; their younger daughter Mary had died of consumption. Anstis, too, was ill. Hannah's father sent her their spaniel Marcus, a maid and a plea: name your conspirators in the elopement, and I'll come and take you home. Her father even made the trip to Providence several times with the intent. But Hannah would not see him, for she would not—could not—reveal that her uncle William and her cousin had helped her.

"Then let the foolish thing die where she is" was her father's response.

Eventually, William Gardiner heard of his niece's predicament and told Rowland he had arranged for Peter to be in the Wickford woods that night. Rowland and William rushed to Providence but arrived too late. Hannah was dying. Her father gathered her things, and they journeyed home. It was June, and the Robinson estate was in its full glory. Hannah asked that the procession stop so that she might enjoy a bird's-eye view of her family's estate. She picked a flower, a withered sprig of life everlasting, and tucked it into her blouse. That night, a whippoorwill, omen of death, sang a dirge on the lilac bush beneath Hannah's window. In the morning, she was dead.

"She got the consumption," the Robinsons' servants told one another.

"No," said her nurse, the witch Mum Amey. "She died of a broken heart."

Hannah Robinson Tower, South Kingstown. *Photo by author.*

Her spaniel Marcus did, too, days later, atop her grave, where he'd kept vigil from the time of her burial. Peter Simons visited his father-in-law once after Hannah's passing. The two never spoke again, and Peter returned to Europe. Rowland Robinson visited his daughter's grave every day until he died.

Hannah Robinson's tombstone, Narragansett. *Photo by author.*

But is Hannah at rest? Some aren't so sure. Not so long ago, two little boys stayed a night in Hannah's room. The next morning, one told his mother he would not sleep in the room again. A lady in white at the foot of his bed kept him up most of the night with her crying.

AN INCIDENT AT DARK SWAMP

Now

Chepachet locals shake their heads and mutter when outsiders ask where to find the Dark Swamp. There's a reason why no roads lead to it and no houses were ever built within two miles of it.

Nature herself seems to want to imprison the swamp. Or something in it. She's done her best to ward off seekers, knitting together brambles, thorns, poison ivy and sumac into a nearly impenetrable barrier. She's stocked the swamp with hoards of tics, snakes and other biting things. She's filled the trees with creatures that screech and howl their warnings to stay out. Stay away.

But still, they come.

You'd think, the townspeople say to one another over a pint at the Stagecoach Tavern, knowing people get lost out there would scare them

Chepachet Historic District sign. *Photo by author.*

Above: The Stagecoach Tavern, Chepachet. *Photo by author*.

Right: Stagecoach Tavern sign, Chepachet. *Photo by author*.

off, but the fools keep coming. Idiots who look like they've never been outside coming to town with their backpacks, their water bottles and trail mix, babbling on about that ridiculous writer Lovecraft and the goddamn swamp.

Truth is, not many people in Chepachet can say where the Dark Swamp is. There are a few who like to have a little fun with the kids. They look over their shoulders, left and then right, fix a stare on them and lower their voices, as if they're revealing a big secret to a chosen few. They say, "Take Route 94 south to Willy Road; it's an old dirt road. Follow it till you come to the very end. You'll see Victory Sportsman's Club. Get out of your car. Take a long look. The Sportsman's Club is private property, and there's no right of way to the swamp. Then, go home, would ya."

Glocester Heritage Society, Chepachet.
Photo by author.

But the damn kids don't. They move on, stop at different restaurants, gas stations, the library or maybe the Glocester Historical Society, looking for the oldest people they can find, hoping that people that ancient will know where to find "IT."

But no one will. They've worked hard to forget—abandoned memories as they abandoned the land. The Dark Swamp, a place so thick with trees and brush that they've grown into one another, branches intertwined and tented like the gnarled fingers of old women in prayer. But there's nothing holy about that place. It's gray, wet, cold and filled with slithering, croaking things. Things that, if given the chance, would wrap themselves around you and draw you down to into the murk.

Then again, maybe the things that kill us are the merciful ones. There's an end to the torment. With your death, you're released.

What if the worst predator is one who lets you live but never lets you go?

Then

It was a quest of the grotesque and terrible—a search for Dark Swamp in Northwestern Rhode Island, of which Eddy had heard sinister whispers among the rusticks. They whisper that it is very remote and very strange, and that no one has ever been completely thro' it because of the treacherous and unfathomable potholes and the ancient trees whose thick boles grow so closely together that passage is difficult and darkness omnipresent even at noon, and other things, of which bobcats—whose half-human howls are heard in the night by peasants near the edge—are the very least.
—H.P. Lovecraft's letter to Frank Belknap Long, November 8, 1923

Howard P. Lovecraft and C.M. Eddy set out to search for the Dark Swamp and IT in November 1923. Approaching middle age, they were too old to be engaged in such a silly act. They were gentlemen, writers. Eddy had a wife and children. Usually, the only people looking for IT were stupid kids searching for a thrill. But these were serious men.

Howard had the look of someone who'd been stretched. He was gangly and awkward with a long face that bore an unfortunate resemblance to

Adolf Hitler's. Eddy—he preferred being addressed by his last name—had a pinched face dominated by a hawkish nose and heavy black eyebrows. If Eddy wasn't smiling, he could appear sinister. However forbidding their appearance, though, their skittishness made them ridiculous. They shivered as tangles of marsh grass and algae's rubbery tendrils clung to their legs; they winced as cold, slithering things brushed against their ankles; and they jumped at the caterwauling and hooting of the creatures in the swamp. But they forged on. They just wanted to have a look at the Dark Swamp. They wanted to glimpse IT for themselves.

Eddy had been the one to hear the story first. He had been in the Chepachet Post Office one night earlier that autumn. He'd told Howard about it on one of their nocturnal rambles through Fox Point.

"Men were gathered round the fire telling hunting tales when someone brought up the Dark Swamp," Eddy said. "They were wondering why all the squirrels and rabbits left the hill and headed to Connecticut."

Brown & Hopkins Country Store, Chepachet. *Photo by author.*

Howard grunted. This was his encouragement to Eddy to continue.

"So there's this grizzled old codger with a gun who says IT has moved into the Dark Swamp. He said he'd seen IT craning its ugly, monstrous head out of a hole to stare at him. He'd drawn his gun on IT and backed away. 'And I swear,' the old man said. 'IT smiled at me. Smiled.'"

"And then?"

Eddy shrugged. "He left. He said, way back in 1849, when he was just a little boy, his grandfather had told him about how the Dark Swamp was the lair of a monster who'd been there since before Roger Williams and even the Indians. He said he hadn't believed his grandfather then, but he did now."

"Did you get his name?" Howard asked.

Eddy smiled.

"He won't take you in. I asked him. He said anyone who went in was a damn fool who deserved his fate."

Howard laughed. "Are you free Sunday?"

They told Eddy's wife, Muriel, that they had research to do. Both were writers of horror, and this was a bona fide monster and a local. Howard had achieved some fame; Eddy had not. Both, no doubt, hoped to discover some wretched being, some Gollum-like character crouched among the weeds.

"Two middle-aged men tromping around a swamp looking for a monster?" Muriel snapped. But her taunts did not deter them.

And so, here they were, out in the woods, half a day spent in search of IT. IT—a thing that eluded definition and identification. If indeed IT were a living thing and not some story told to keep children in their beds, how should the monster be handled? What would IT look like? Would IT be some huge, slithering, fanged thing, or would IT be invisible, a ghost?

Howard thought he saw something—a shadow?—flit between the trees ahead of him as he and Eddy walked into what they believed was the Dark Swamp. The thing was dark and legless, with tendrils tapering to nothingness. Howard struggled through the muck; with every footstep, he battled to be free of the sucking mud. He whispered an urgent order for Eddy, who'd fallen behind, to follow. Howard heard the splash a moment later. It was too loud. Too loud to be a beaver or a bullfrog.

He turned to see that Eddy had fallen off their narrow path and landed, facedown, in swamp water. He struggled against marsh grass, duckweed and muck to get back to his friend. Howard pulled Eddy from the water onto more stable mud. Eddy's face was slimy with duckweed and muck. He knelt beside Eddy. Was he breathing? Howard placed his ear to his friend's chest. There was the slightest movement. He was breathing, slowly, peacefully, strangely for a man who had just been facedown in water. Howard shook Eddy, but it was as if he were asleep. He stood and looked around. There was nothing but swamp and menacing woods all around them.

"Oh, God," Howard muttered, though in truth he didn't believe in God. But he also didn't believe in his own ability to get his friend and himself out of this mess. And the afternoon sun was waning. Howard shivered. How long would either of them survive out here?

IT came to him then. The first assault: IT attacked his mind. Visions of horrid creatures; shifting, formless demons of nightmares; things that slither behind walls, that rise in noxious vapors from basement floors, that seep out of potholes, that swoop down from the night sky to scoop you up in their talons and their beaks—these are the things that came to roost in his mind. And he knew he was not their creator, that those grotesque, vile, monstrous things that would, if real, strip a man of his sanity were given to him by something very old, very evil and very real.

And they were never leaving him. It was an unbidden thought and certain truth; Howard knew it.

Howard sobbed now. Was he, too, to lose his mind, like his mother and father before him? Was this how madness worked? Tears and snot ran over his lips and into the corners of his mouth. He swiped his sleeve across his face and succeeded only in adding duckweed and mud to the mix. He felt a hot stream of urine course down his leg.

"Please," he said.

Then came the second assault: contact. Howard could feel the thing's breath upon his ear. It was all around him now, a presence that felt like a fish, like a squid, all cold, wet arms and tentacles, plucking, pulling, fixing on him. He felt ill. Breathed heavily. Feared he would pass out. And in that moment, he thought death just might be a blessing. A way to escape this thing that, he realized, had always been lurking around him, revealing itself in his nightmares. His Night Gaunt was real.

This is what madness feels like.

And then IT was gone. At least, the feeling of IT against him was gone. But IT would never really be gone, Howard knew. IT was in him now, a part of him.

In despair, Howard sank to his knees, by the body of his friend, and cried. Howard felt Eddy jerk and then cough. Eddy opened his eyes and looked around.

"What happened?"

Howard lifted his head up. "You fell facedown into the swamp. You weren't breathing. I thought you were dead."

Eddy sat up. "I don't remember."

Howard cupped brackish water in his hands and scrubbed his face, composing himself. When he was done, he turned to Eddy.

"We need to get out of here."

"Yes, it'll be dark very soon."

The two men were surprised to find that the way out seemed to take a fraction of the time it had taken them to wade in. Also missed on their way in was a small farmhouse. The two bedraggled gentlemen approached the house and were warmly received. The missus was a fan of Lovecraft. The farmer gave them warm clothing, and his wife served them gingerbread and milk. Eddy explained their purpose for being in the area. The husband and wife exchanged looks, laughed and shook their heads.

"Yes, the swamp that sees no sun. The monster that lives there," the farmer said. "We've heard it all, of course. People disappearing. We figure it must be somebody's idea of a joke. You know, a scary story like the ones your ma would tell you to warn you off of misbehaving. There's plenty of swamps around here, to be sure. And sometimes cows go missing in the swamplands, but most get found."

Howard said nothing. Eddy chatted more with the couple before thanking them for their hospitality and ushering his friend out the door and into the car. Howard was wan, pale and uncommunicative. Eddy feared he'd somehow offended his friend. Howard was unequivocally odd.

"I'm sorry, Howard, that this was such a wasted day," Eddy said. "We can come back. Next week, maybe?"

"No," said Howard. "There's nothing out there. Not anymore."

LAIR OF THE LOUP GAROU

When Pierre and his brothers were very, very good, if they'd done their chores and said their prayers, then their father would tell them the stories of his childhood in Canada, a land where snow stayed all year round and beasts were bigger than men.

And sometimes men were beasts.

"Tell us of the loup garou," they would beg their father. And their father would roll his eyes and make the sign of the cross. He would have them check the locks on their little home's doors and windows. He'd take a candle and shine it in the shadowy recesses of the boys' room. The loup garou loved darkness, he would tell his boys.

"Did they really follow you here, to Woonsocket?" Pierre asked his father. Pierre was the oldest boy, and it was his duty to doubt his father's stories.

Father frowned at him.

"Yes," he said as he cocooned each boy in blankets. Arms and legs left untucked were bound to be grabbed by things that lived under the bed. "The werewolves, the loups garous, as we call them, they were with us when we came to America. We didn't know, of course. They appear as men. And sometimes women. They look like us; they act like us. But they are not us."

Charles, the littlest, wriggled with terror and excitement.

"They are the devil's children. Bad men and women whose evil has bound them to him. And he has cursed them, made them loups garous. Man eaters."

"Can they be killed, Papa?" Giles, the middle son, asked.

"Yes," said Father. "They can be killed. If you stab them with a knife until they bleed, they will die. But they are strong, and it is not easy. Most who try, die. You must kill them before they kill you."

Werewolf von Neuses, circa 1685. *PD-US.*

Father shivered.

"If you hear rumor of a loup garou prowling our woods, you watch the shadows, keep a light in hand," Pierre's father told him. "They keep to the shadows, until they attack."

From their father's stories, the boys fashioned games. Pierre and his brothers dared one another to look in the shadows and played Pierce the Loup Garou with sticks, taking turns as the monster, chasing one another, running from their mother and her switch when she caught them at it. She was afraid they would hurt themselves. They thought it wise not to point out that the switch hurt more than the poke of a stick.

When they grew, Pierre and his brothers exchanged their stick swords for axes and plows to help their father hew lumber and till fields. And alongside the forgotten toys and games of youth, they placed their father's bedtime stories.

Until the night Father fell ill.

He'd been out of sorts all day. His back and legs hurt him in the winters. But that night, the pain was much more severe than usual. He fell into fits, frothing at the mouth, eyes running and body quaking as if electrified.

Pierre feared his father was under attack by spirits and headed out to fetch the local priest. It was winter, so he took the sleigh and the family's strongest, fastest horse. They flew through the night, moving so quickly that Pierre thought at times they were taking flight. Soon, he saw the lights of the village ahead and the iron gate of the priest's cottage.

If the priest were awake, he could get him back to the farmhouse within the hour. Pierre relaxed just a little and nearly fell from the sleigh entirely when the wolf latched onto the back of it.

It was the size of a man. The wolf's forepaws curled over the back of the sleigh's seat as it scrambled with its hind legs to get to Pierre. The screech of claws on metal and the wolf's howling caused the horse to rear up and nearly topple the sleigh. Pierre snapped his reins and shouted at the horse. With his free hand, he tried to take the whip to the wolf, but it was too long and the wolf was too close.

The monster bared its teeth and snapped at Pierre, who dodged his dripping maw while urging his horse forward. And for a moment, Pierre looked back and saw the eyes not of a beast but of a man. He could have sworn he saw the wolf grin.

But the wolf's leer was replaced by a hateful look and followed by a long, low growl. Pierre's horse had run through the gate, and Pierre, sleigh and wolf were now in the priest's yard. The priest was there, shouting words Pierre did not understand. The wolf, which moments before had been so close that Pierre felt its muzzle on the back of his neck, fell from the sleigh, screaming in a voice clearly human. Pierre turned to see a naked man scrambling on all fours in his haste to be free of the priest.

The boy fainted then, fear and exhaustion overcoming him. When Pierre awoke, he was back in his home. His father, his mother told him, had returned to health and barely recalled the pain and fits of the night before. Pierre, though, recalled the events of that night for the remainder of his days.

MRS. JENCKS'S GHOST

Long ago, in days when wolves and bears roamed the woods of Scituate, weary travelers would take refuge for the night in the Black Horse Tavern. For the most part, they received decent food and comfortable lodging for their money.

But some may have been better off taking their chances with the beasts of the night rather than letting a room at the Black Horse.

There was one room in the tavern that could be had more cheaply than the rest. Still, it remained vacant much of the time. It was called the Indian Room, for the ghost of a Native American brave was reported to haunt it. Some said that in life this brave was the faithful servant of the proprietor of a rival inn, the Pine Tree Inn, and had vowed to haunt the Black Horse to force its closure. Others said that this wasn't the ghost's motive at all. Among those who thought differently were the tavern's owners, Mr. and Mrs. Jencks.

Reuben Jencks was an older man, fat and loud, with a slight fringe of hair ringed around his otherwise bald head. Lucy was much younger, an Irish beauty with delicate features and hair as red as fire. They'd just

Tavern sign. *Photo by author.*

arrived one night in October, when the weather turned cold and sleeping outside became uncomfortable. That first night the Jenckses stayed at the Black Horse, they laughed at the proprietor's warnings about the Indian Room. They didn't believe in ghosts. They did, however, believe in taking advantage of a good deal when they heard of one. And they figured a good tale of terror would buy them free lodging and breakfast come morning, warning or no warning.

And so they bedded down and slept peacefully. Until they didn't.

Mrs. Jencks awoke in the night to find her head bare. Her cap was missing. In its place was a hand twisting her long, red hair into a knot and pulling. She screamed at her husband to light the kerosene lamp by the bed as she struggled with the man—for it was a man's hand, of that much she was sure. Her husband lit the lamp, looked at her, looked beyond her and scrambled out of bed. He pressed his back to wall of the small chamber. Mrs. Jencks's terror grew at the sight of her husband's face, ghastly in lamplight. He was praying.

"Help me!" she screamed.

Then she saw him in the mirror. He was behind her. A tall, fierce young man, his handsome face streaked with tears. Mrs. Jencks struggled, trying to pry his hand from her hair. She had reason to fear for her scalp. The brave held a tomahawk in his free hand. But there it stayed. He roped her long hair once more around his wrist and jerked Mrs. Jencks to her feet. He pulled her across the room. He kicked the door open and, still holding her hair, dragged her down the tavern stairs and out the door. Once outside, he forced Mrs. Jencks to her knees and pulled her hair back and down so that she bent, spine arched, her uplifted face looking into his. The brave swung the tomahawk above his head. Mrs. Jencks heard her husband yell, "No!" She closed her eyes, unwilling to watch the tomahawk's descent into her scalp or perhaps her throat. She felt her whole body shudder. And then, nothing.

She heard a noise then, the thwack of blade hitting wood. She opened her eyes. In the moonlight, she saw the tomahawk, its head buried in the bark of the great cedar tree at the tavern gate.

The brave let go of her then. Mrs. Jencks fell backward into the dirt.

He muttered something about revenge and taking back what was his. He shook Mrs. Jencks, staring into her eyes with such intensity that she went limp and mute. Then he disappeared.

The next day, when the couple related what had happened, the tavern owner, a man named Charles, nodded wearily and set down a plate of bread and bacon for them both. There'd be no charge for their stay, Charles told the couple. He would provide them with a new room if they desired.

"No," Mrs. Jencks said. "We want that room."

Charles gaped at Mrs. Jencks. Her right eye was swollen shut and bruised purple, her lower lip split. She was favoring one foot over the other, likely due to a twisted ankle or some other injury common to someone dragged down several flights of stairs. The sight of Mrs. Jencks had convinced him it was time to do as the Indian brave wanted and close the tavern once and for all. And here she was saying she would stay. "I don't understand," Charles said.

"We want to stay. In fact, we want to buy the Black Horse. We'll pay you well."

"And you?" Charles addressed Mr. Jencks now.

The man shrugged. "There's no changing her mind once she's settled it."

Charles happily rid himself of the inn. He'd been wanting to be free of the godforsaken place, and this couple knew exactly what they were getting. But he stayed on, managing it for the couple, because they weren't interested in running it themselves. Mrs. Jencks's beatings kept them up most of the night, and their days were devoted to, of all things, gardening.

Over time, the Black Horse became a local showpiece for its flower beds and enormous vegetable garden. But the tavern itself was in financial ruin. No one wanted to hear Mrs. Jencks's screaming night after night. Charles knew there must be a reason why she took it. But Mrs. Jencks kept her reasons to herself.

It went on for years this way. And the Jenckses changed. Lucy Jencks's copper hair threaded with silver. Mr. Jencks lost his portly figure. The few out-of-town guests who let rooms never stayed long. They did not like how the Jenckses crept about the inn and the property. Then one day, Mr. Jencks was gone. But it did not seem to bother Mrs. Jencks. She just continued on.

Until the morning Charles found his employer asleep outdoors, shivering in her nightdress under an apple tree. Her fingernails were black with dirt. She'd been clawing at the flower bed beneath the tree. The innkeeper roused Mrs. Jencks, wrapped her in a blanket and brought her inside. He gave her coffee laced with brandy.

Perhaps it was the liquor. Perhaps it was his kindness. Perhaps it was her despair. Whatever the reason, Mrs. Jencks finally shared her secret. She told him of the Indian brave, the tomahawk and the cedar tree. The innkeeper nodded. He'd heard it all before.

"But what you don't understand, what I believe is, there is treasure on this land," Mrs. Jencks said. "And I believe the Indian boy is trying to tell me where it is, but he's not even sure where. Night after night he drags me from my bed to the yard and drives his tomahawk into a different tree—the great cedar, the fine apple, the birch. Mr. Jencks would dig wherever his tomahawk landed, but there was never anything.

"We covered our tracks with flower beds so that you would not suspect us," she said. She put her forehead on the table where she sat, palms pressed into its boards. "You've been so kind, better to me than my good-for-nothing husband, and I've repaid you by trying to steal from you what was rightfully yours.

"My husband said he was tired of digging for nothing. But I know, I know," she said. "He is trying to tell me, to show me something."

Charles shook his head. "All these years, I haven't seen you without a bruise since the first night you walked into the inn."

Mrs. Jencks shook her head violently.

"He's not ever hurt me, not really. He's just desperate to show me. And I will keep looking for as long as he chooses to guide me."

And so she did. For many, many years. An old wig and a hairless doll were all the treasure she ever found for her troubles.

NARRAGANSETT: THE LOST ATLANTIS

Thomas Hazard was weary. World-weary. He'd lost his wife, Fanny, and his five girls. Only he and Barclay remained now. It was for his son that Thomas lived. The only thing worse than his own fate would be his son's if the boy were to lose his father, too.

Thomas looked everywhere for his wife. In crystal balls and tarot cards, runes, dice and tea leaves; in ministers and magicians, priests, mediums, witches, seers, medicine men and wise women. He looked for omens in the stars, in the sand, in the waves, in crystals and in the palms of his own hands.

But there was nothing.

Today, a seagull held his gaze. In its beak was a randy crab, its claws waving in wrath at its capture, angling for but always missing the bird's golden eyes. The bird edged closer to Thomas—clearly it had decided that he posed less of a threat than his own kind, a half dozen more like himself, perched just ashore on a rock, cursing his good fortune, looking for the chance to steal his breakfast from him.

Thomas couldn't help himself. Was the bird there for him? Was there meaning to be derived from something so ordinary? The bird cocked its head and looked at him quizzically, it seemed. Fanny had loved birds. Not gulls, especially, but other ocean birds, such as plovers. More elegant, feminine things, as Fanny herself had been. He was the gull: big, brash, a prankster, ever ready for a good fight.

There was no way this gull bore a message from the afterlife. It was wishful thinking, something even his old nurse, an ignorant but loving woman, would have laughed at. She who had told him Worden's Pond was the province of fairies who would dance by moonlight in the olden times when Narragansett bore another name and the gods and goddesses summered here. When it was Atlantis.

Atlantis? Yes, Atlantis, the Greek island that sank into the sea and resurfaced under a new name: Narragansett.

Thomas sighed and hung his head. He imagined he looked pathetic, a lonely figure, hunched and broken, a snail clinging to Flat Rock, his only company a gray and grizzled fisherman a few flat rocks to the south, threading a hook through the head of an eel.

A view from Hazard Avenue, Narragansett. *Photo by author.*

Another view from Hazard Avenue, Narragansett. *Photo by author.*

October is just the most divine month in the whole twelve months of the year in Rhode Island, especially along the southern coast of its vast domain, which was formerly known as Atlantis, the delightful summer resort of the gods and goddesses of antiquity.

A strange thought. Thomas closed his eyes and shook his head. But the gods weren't done with him yet.

He opened his eyes.

Though the sun still shone, the ocean was roiling. There was Neptune, the god of sea and horses, bare-chested and fishing where the old man had been a moment before. Trident in hand, Neptune harpooned one five-hundred-pound porpoise after another. Vaulting onto his trident, the porpoises appeared to welcome their fate. Neptune pulled them from his trident and flung them in the direction of Point Judith with such speed and violence that the air rained with their reentry into the Salt Pond.

Next came Apollo, holding in his right hand a bow and arrows and in his left, a shield and harp. Around his shoulders he wore a coiled fishing line. He placed his shield and harp on a rock. The harp immediately began to play as the god of rhetoric, music and poetry started fishing. While Neptune worked alone, Apollo brought an entourage: nine gorgeous women playing instruments and singing siren songs so powerful that all the fish in the sea leapt in ecstasy. Apollo cast his golden sinker and hook into the water and effortlessly reeled in a two-hundred-pound bass.

Postcard of King Neptune. *Library of Congress.*

Apollo and the Muses by Baldassare Peruzzi.

Neptune and Apollo's antics were but a prelude. There, on the horizon, was a regatta led by the goddess Aurora, coming from the east on a gold chariot drawn by white horses. Their hooves did not make the slightest impression on the water.

After Aurora came a parade of gods. "All the celestial and terrestrial gods and goddesses and their numerous retinues, together with the gods of the woods and the sea, not even excluding the infernal gods, led on by Pluto (who, however, I observed, were, for some cause, required by Jupiter to keep within the boundaries of Massachusetts, in Buzzard's Bay)," Hazard later told friends.

Mars held a tournament on Narragansett Beach, and Venus hosted a closing reception with her trainbearer, Adonis, two cupids and three graces.

Thomas listened to the music of a million fairies, birds and angels, the score of a mock battle between Jupiter, Neptune and Aeolus. Jupiter and Aeolus conjured wind and lightning, forcing the sea back ten miles, leaving its inhabitants struggling in the open air.

The gods laughed at the sight and restored the ocean in one giant wave so forceful that Jupiter was thrown from his thundercloud. Thomas watched, mouth open, as the god of lightning landed on Jimmy Robinson's sand hill north of the pier.

Facedown in the sand, the great god sprawled, flattened like a bullfrog. Thomas laughed to see the town drunk, Jim Phillips, trip over Jupiter and then haul him up by the armpits. Old Jim tried to brush the sand

Narragansett Beach. *Photo by author.*

free from the god, but ungrateful Jupiter batted him away as if he were a horsefly. The other gods and goddesses laughed to see Jupiter so humbled, and the noise was seismic. Thomas pressed his hands to his ears. Blinked. And then all were gone.

Except the grizzled fisherman, who grinned knowingly at Thomas. He threw his arms up, pole in one hand and fish in the other. Neptune incognito.

Thomas smiled—a sign.

SHE WHO SHALL NOT BE NAMED

From the bogs of Swamptown, in the wild woods of Kettle Hole and Hell Hollow, comes this story of a lovelorn witch.

The object of her affection was one Charles H. Rose of Kettle Hole. Charles was a rare man, a successful mill owner who also read the Greek Testament and wrote poetry. A hermit, he preferred the company of animals to people. He ate no pork and did not drink or smoke. A devout Episcopalian, he enjoyed debating the Second Adventists about the second coming of Christ.

Not the usual consort for a servant of Satan, to be sure.

So what was it about Charles Rose that charmed the witch? It must be that another witch cast a spell for, surely, a woman who celebrated her Sabbath by stripping and dancing with spirits under the full moon could not fall in love with a Bible-loving Christian man voluntarily.

Whether it was love or magic that moved the witch, it was certainly powerful. So powerful that she left Hell Hollow and paid a visit to Charles, whereupon she proposed that they marry. She had no dowry to speak of, but she could cast spells, brew potions, hex enemies and predict futures. Surely that would be appealing to an entrepreneurial sort like Charles.

Magic and mayhem were her stock and trade. But Charles wasn't in the market for magic or a woman.

He refused the witch's proposal. And she pined for him until she died.

But witches don't really die. They shed their skins, becoming pure spirit. Some are allowed to roam the earth doing the devil's work, becoming the familiars of living witches. Never, ever are they to be called by name after death, for to do so is to summon them. The people who knew the witch who loved Charles Rose knew this, and they never uttered her name after her passing. And so Charles's sorceress's name is forgotten. But she left an impression, nonetheless. Her epitaph reads:

This old _____ _____
Has danced her jig,
She'll never dance no more
She's gone to hell,
Where devils dwell
Upon the fiery shore.

WATCHING AND WAITING FOR YOU

The old woman sat on the hard, wooden chair, rubbing her gnarled hands together, wincing with pain. Rain was coming. Her joints swelled in anticipation. The old woman wished she could go back to bed, but she knew that thing wouldn't let her. Not until she'd done what she must do.

She hunched over her typewriter. Her eyesight was poor, and the light from her single lamp did little to ward off the dark. There was nothing—no noise to break the silence at this hour. The old woman shivered as she looked out her window. Neither stars nor moon to illuminate the creature that surely stood there. Watching her. Waiting for her.

It had seemed such a harmless thing, what she'd done. It was more than forty years ago now. She'd been a young teacher then. She'd taught high school in Coventry. History. It was Halloween, and her students were impossible. She'd had a fun lesson planned—at least, she thought it fun. The class was studying Elizabethan England. She and the students would act out the scene from *Macbeth* where he met the witches. "Double, double toil and trouble. Fire burn, and cauldron bubble" and all of that "eye of newt, toe of frog" stuff.

But the kids wouldn't focus, and she was aggravated. Ten minutes to the end of class, she gave up on Shakespeare.

"How would you like to hear the story of a real witch and vampire?" she asked.

The kids, most of them, stopped their conversations. Encouraged, she continued.

"You know, some say there's a vampire right in West Greenwich."

"I know the story," one kid began.

"Shush, let her tell it."

"Well, a long time ago, in the late 1800s, there was a young girl, nineteen or twenty, who died of a terrible wasting disease. Some said it was pneumonia, some said tuberculosis. They buried her in the cemetery by the little church she attended. But after she died, strange things started happening to other children in her town. They started complaining that the dead girl visited them at night. That she would sit on their chests and suck the air from their lungs or draw blood from their lips.

West Greenwich Baptist Church sign. *Photo by author.*

"The children started getting sick, wasting away like the girl had and, eventually, dying. The parents in the village were afraid that their children weren't dying of some disease but that they were being fed upon."

No noise in the room now.

"So the town fathers decided that they would dig up the girl's body and rip out her heart. They believed if they did this, the vampire—whom they thought resided in the heart—would be destroyed."

A hand flew up in the back of the room. "Did they really dig her up and cut her open?"

"Yes, they did," the teacher said.

"And did it stop?"

"No. The children kept dying. You see, you can't kill what's already dead. Your only defense against such things is to read the signs and keep away. Some say vampires can't stray too far from their graves. And there were signs. No grass would grow on her grave. And then there was her headstone."

"What? What did the headstone say?"

She paused a moment and then intoned: "I Am Waiting and Watching for You."

There was a little scream and some laughter at this.

"What does that mean?"

"Well, some say it's her warning to her victims. If you should go visit her, well, you've agreed to be dinner."

"I'm so gonna find this place!" one of the male students in the class yelled. He high-fived another student.

The teacher shook her head. "Don't go getting yourself in trouble over a silly story. If you go toppling headstones, you'll be in trouble with more than just your parents. And there's a legend about messing with vampires' headstones, too."

The bell rang, interrupting any further discussion.

"What's the name of the girl?" one student asked as they filed out.

"I don't know," she said. "And even if I did, I wouldn't tell you. I don't want anyone camping out in old graveyards this Halloween."

And that was the end of it. For more than twenty years.

The day the horror began started simply enough. She was called into the principal's office. There sat a lady from the local historical society whose grandchild, she said, had told her a ghost story. The same ghost story the teacher had been telling for years: "I Am Watching and Waiting for You."

"You've been spreading that terrible tale, my granddaughter tells me," the old woman said.

"Yes, I've been telling that story on and off for twenty years. I'm sorry. Did it scare your granddaughter?"

The old woman's powdered face flushed red with anger.

"It's just a harmless ghost story to entertain kids at Halloween. An old ghost story my father told me," the teacher said to the old lady with the rheumy, red-rimmed eyes.

"Well, you got your tales mixed up. Nellie Vaughn is no vampire." The woman wagged a bony finger at her. "And now we've got kids breaking off pieces of her headstone and trying to dig her up!"

"I'm sorry, but I've never mentioned any Nellie Vaughn. I don't know any Nellie Vaughn. I never knew whom the story was about."

"But you knew about the inscription and you told them that, didn't you?" The old woman was beginning to sound menacing.

The teacher looked to her principal. His hands were tented, and his chin rested on them. This was his standard I'm-really-concentrating-on-what-you're-saying posture he reserved for students and their parents. He'd be of no help to her.

"I'd heard there was a graveyard with a headstone with that inscription. But you have to understand, if you know a bit about old headstones, that's not an unusual inscription. It was often used on the headstones of people who died young. It meant that they were looking out for the family they left on earth and that they'd be waiting for them in heaven. It's only out of context that it sounds scary."

The old woman shook her head and sighed the sigh of someone made to suffer a fool.

"I know what the inscription means, but your students don't, and now they've gone and desecrated a grave. And you're to blame."

"I am sorry, but you can't blame me for what kids—I mean, do we even know that they're my students?—may or may not have done in a graveyard that I couldn't even get them to because I don't know where the headstone even is!"

"Well, that's just more irresponsibility on your part," the old woman said. "You're a history teacher, I'm told. Why don't you stick to that and leave the gossiping to your students. It's shameful what you've done!"

The principal and the teacher stood as the old woman gathered her things—an umbrella and an old patent-leather purse. She walked to the door of the principal's office, opened it and then paused. She turned.

"I've managed to undo some of your mischief," the old woman spat. "The church has removed the headstone and hidden it away. In time, the location of Nellie's grave will be forgotten. Grass and weeds will take care of the rest. And she'll be spared further degradation.

Then she smiled. It wasn't a friendly smile.

"Since you're so enamored of superstition, you might find this interesting," she said. "Some believe the headstone is there to tether what lies beneath it. The vampire will only roam so far because she is bound to return to it. But when you remove the headstone of a witch or vampire, you make it impossible for her to find her final resting place. You could say she's doomed to wander without rest for all eternity.

"Or you could say you've set her loose."

The old woman shook her head.

"Let's hope Nellie isn't a vampire, or she may just come looking for you."

The teacher made a joke of the old woman, "The Hag," to anyone who'd listen. Laughter helped keep her unease at bay. For though she was very rational woman, she couldn't stop thinking about what the old woman had said. It got so that she felt chilled at the memory of their conversation and guilty that Nellie's headstone had been removed. Not, she told herself, because she believed a vampire roamed the woods of West Greenwich but rather because she'd taken the one last bit of evidence that there'd ever been a Nellie Vaughn.

Now that she had the vampire's identity, finding the cemetery was easy. She visited on a cold autumn day with an armful of hothouse flowers in hand. Of course, she couldn't be sure of the exact location of the grave because the headstone had been removed. But there was a spot between two headstones that was a little sunken and, where there was grass elsewhere, here there was more of a growth, not lichen, but like it—a yellow-green growth that she recoiled from without knowing why. She gently tossed the flowers, forget-me-nots, baby's breath and life everlasting, where she thought the headstone would be.

A voice from behind made her jump.

"Those are very pretty."

Plain Meeting House, West Greenwich. *Photo by author.*

Plain Meeting House Road sign, West Greenwich. *Photo by author.*

She turned to see a lovely young girl, thin and pale, in a modest blouse and skirt, the kind you might see in a Merchant-Ivory movie or at a Baptist church. The girl's hair was bound in a neat braid. The teacher had seen such girls at a church near her house and thought them quaint. Envied them a little, even. The waistband of her own skirt, an A-line, felt tight. So much sin could be hidden with modest clothing like hers.

"What are you doing?" the girl asked.

The teacher's mind raced. How to explain herself? I'm a silly middle-aged woman afraid I've angered a vampire so I'm tossing flowers on her grave? "I'm a teacher, and I told this ghost story about a girl buried here a long time ago. And I've learned that because of the story, this poor girl's headstone had to be removed. Kids were trampling on her grave and chipping away at the headstone. I feel terrible about it."

The girl nodded slowly.

"I've even heard that some have tried to dig up her grave. All because of me. So now, the congregation here has removed her headstone to try to preserve what's left of it, and it strikes me as so wrong. I mean, I understand protecting the headstone, but there's nothing left of her now, nothing to mark her time on earth. I feel I have to do something to make up for it."

The teacher laughed self-consciously.

"Sorry. Sometimes I get a little melodramatic, a little too Edgar Allan Poe."

The girl shook her head.

"I don't think what you're doing sounds silly at all. I think it's the right thing to do," the girl said. "May I make a suggestion?"

The teacher nodded.

"I think you should tell people what you've told me. Tell them you were just telling a harmless story. Tell them there's no vampire here. Tell them Nellie Vaughn was no vampire."

The teacher nodded vigorously. "Yes, I will. I'll do that," she said, drawing her coat close and glancing around her. The temperature had dropped, and the wind had picked up. The day was drawing to a close; the trees' shadows had grown long. She looked at the girl again. She wasn't dressed warmly enough for a late fall day.

"Need a ride?"

The girl looked intently at her, saying nothing. The teacher felt colder still. There was something about the way she looked. Gaunt. Hungry.

"Tell them I am perfectly pleasant."

"Excuse me?"

"Tell them Nellie Vaughn is no vampire. Tell them I am perfectly pleasant."

The teacher felt fear now. She stepped backward, away from the girl and the grave. Clearly, the girl was not all there. She turned.

The girl was in front of her now.

The teacher screamed—just once—and crossed herself.

"When they took the stone away, I didn't know what I would do," the girl said. Her eyes were wide with remembering. "Before, I could count on a few coming to see me every so often. It was enough to get by."

"But now they don't know where to find me," she said and frowned. "They've stopped coming. It was so easy before. Now I'm so hungry, so weak. And so weary. I can't rest."

The teacher shuddered.

"So you will continue what you've started," the girl said. "You will continue to keep my story, and me," she smiled at this, "alive." You will tell them where to find me." The girl grinned now, displaying delicate, needle-like teeth. "You'll tell them I'm not a vampire. And they will come. To see for themselves."

"No," the teacher said.

"Oh, you will," Nellie said. "If you wish to continue living."

And that was the beginning of it. Twenty years ago.

The teacher clenched her arthritic hands and whimpered in frustration. And fear. Then she began to type: "Dear Editor: I am writing to dispute the story you printed in your Oct. 30 story 'Nellie Vaughn: Vampire.' There is absolutely no historical evidence to support that Nellie Vaughn was a vampire…"

Selected Bibliography

Bacon, Edgar Mayhew. *Narragansett Bay: Its Historic and Romantic Associations and Picturesque Setting*. New York: G.P. Putnam's Sons, 1904.

Brennan, J.T. *Ghosts of Newport: Spirits, Scoundrels, Legends and Lore*. Charleston, SC: Haunted America, 2007.

Earle, Alice Morse. *In Old Narragansett: Romances and Realities*. New York: C. Scribner's Sons, 1898.

Hazard, Caroline. *Anchors of Tradition: A Presentment of Some Little-Known Facts and Persons in a Small Corner of Colonial New England Called Narragansett, to Which Are Added Certain Weavings of Fancy from the Thread of Life upon the Loom of Time*. New Haven: Yale University Press, 1924.

Hazard, Thomas R. *The Jonnycake Papers of Shepherd Tom: Together with Reminiscences of Narragansett Schools of Former Days*. Boston: Merrymount, 1915.

Hazard, Thomas R., and Willis P. Hazard. *Recollections of Olden Times: Rowland Robinson of Narragansett and His Unfortunate Daughter: with Genealogies of the Robinson, Hazard, and Sweet Families of Rhode Island/by Thomas R. Hazard. Also, Genealogical Sketch of the Hazards of the Middle States*. Newport, RI: J.P. Sanborne, 1879.

The Legend of Carbuncle Pond. Providence, RI: Old Stone Bank, 1931.

Livermore, S.T. *Livermore's History of Block Island, Rhode Island*. Block Island, RI: Block Island Historical Society, 1961.

New York Times. "Theodore M. Davis, Egyptologist, Dead." February 24, 1915. Available online.

Palmer, Henrietta R., C.R. Williams, David Buffum, Caroline Hazard, Nora Perry and Harriette Potter Richardson. *Rhode Island Tales: Depicting Social Life during the Colonial, Revolutionary and Post-Revolutionary Era*. New York: Purdy, 1928.

Rhode Island: *A Guide to the Smallest State*. Boston: Houghton Mifflin, 1937.

Ritchie, Ethel Colt. *Block Island: Lore and Legends*. Block Island, RI: Frederick N. Ritchie, 1956.

Schlosser, S.E. *Spooky New England: Tales of Hauntings, Strange Happenings, and Other Local Lore*. Guilford, CT: Globe Pequot, 2004.

Simmons, William S. *Spirit of the New England Tribes: Indian History and Folklore*. Hanover, NH: University Press of New England, 1986.

Tinney, Harle H. *The Ghosts of Belcourt Castle*. New York: IUniverse, 2010.

About the Author

M.E. Reilly-McGreen is the author of two previous History Press books: *Witches, Wenches and Wild Women of Rhode Island* and *Revolutionaries, Rebels and Rogues of Rhode Island*. She lives in the Ocean State with her husband and three sons.

Photo by Mark Kiely.

Visit us at
www.historypress.net